Food and Social Media

AltaMira Studies in Food and Gastronomy

General Editor: Ken Albala, Professor of History, University of the Pacific (kalbala@pacific.edu)

AltaMira Executive Editor: Wendi Schnaufer (wschnaufer@rowman.com)

Food Studies is a vibrant and thriving field encompassing not only cooking and eating habits but issues such as health, sustainability, food safety, and animal rights. Scholars in disciplines as diverse as history, anthropology, sociology, literature, and the arts focus on food. The mission of **AltaMira Studies in Food and Gastronomy** is to publish the best in food scholarship, harnessing the energy, ideas, and creativity of a wide array of food writers today. This broad line of food-related titles will range from food history, interdisciplinary food studies monographs, general interest series, and popular trade titles to textbooks for students and budding chefs, scholarly cookbooks, and reference works.

Titles in the Series

Appetites and Aspirations in Vietnam: Food and Drink in the Long Nineteenth Century, by Erica J. Peters
Three World Cuisines: Italian, Mexican, Chinese, by Ken Albala

Food and Social Media

You Are What You Tweet

Signe Rousseau

ALTAMIRA
PRESS

A division of
ROWMAN & LITTLEFIELD PUBLISHERS, INC.
Lanham • New York • Toronto • Plymouth, UK

TX
643
.R68
2012

Published by AltaMira Press
A division of The Rowman & Littlefield Publishing Group, Inc.
A wholly owned subsidiary of The Rowman & Littlefield Publishing Group, Inc.
4501 Forbes Boulevard, Suite 200, Lanham, Maryland 20706
www.rowman.com

10 Thornbury Road, Plymouth PL6 7PP, United Kingdom

British Library Cataloguing in Publication Information Available

Library of Congress Cataloging-in-Publication Data
Rousseau, Signe, 1975– .
Food and social media : you are what you tweet / Signe Rousseau.
p. cm.
Includes bibliographical references.
ISBN 978-0-7591-2042-6 (cloth : alk. paper)—ISBN 978-0-7591-2043-3 (pbk.: alk. paper)—ISBN
978-0-7591-2044-0 (electronic)
1. Cooking—Information services. 2. Social media. 3. Online social networks. 4. Food—Social
aspects. I. Title.
TX643.R68 2012
641.3—dc23
2012005208

⊖™ The paper used in this publication meets the minimum requirements of American
National Standard for Information Sciences Permanence of Paper for Printed Library
Materials, ANSI/NISO Z39.48-1992.

Printed in the United States of America

Contents

Acknowledgments

No book is a solo effort, and certainly not one that relies on the daily activities of millions of mostly unknown people for its subject. This book would not have been possible without the encouragements of Ken Albala and Wendi Schnaufer at AltaMira Press. I met Ken after joining the Association for the Study of Food and Society (ASFS), quite easily the most rewarding group to be a part of for anyone with a scholarly interest of food. I thank its listserv members for continuing to provide stimulating discussions about all things food on a daily basis. Thanks also to JP Rossouw, professional restaurant critic and my brother-in-law, for many interesting conversations about restaurant reviewing and foodie shenanigans. And to his brother: my husband, personal tech geek, and quite simply the best man.

Introduction

A Sweet but Sticky Web

For anyone with a professional or academic interest in food, social media have made the task of both finding and publishing information phenomenally easy. The same can, of course, be said for anyone with a personal interest in food, be it cooking, eating out, or any other aspect of food that one can think of—and probably a good few aspects of food that one would not even have been able to imagine. Anyone with a computer, smartphone, and Internet access can publish recipes, review restaurants, or host a site that features videos, for example, of people crying while eating (http://cryingwhileeating.com). For those who do it well enough to get people's attention, there are ample rewards: publicity through website traffic (sometimes driven by "link love"), virtual and real community recognition, awards, and perhaps the opportunity to turn a hobby into a livelihood. From this perspective, the Web is the great equalizer and a wonderful place to play. But it can also be an unfriendly and deeply unsettling place.

Imagine the following scenario: after an unsatisfactory meal at a restaurant, S. goes home and posts a review of her experience on Yelp (the crowd-sourced review site that led her to the restaurant in the first place, so she considers it appropriate to add her own feedback). The owner of said restaurant comes across the review and, (falsely) informed by his staff that S. neglected to leave a tip for her server, decides to post her picture on the restaurant's Facebook page with this comment: "NOT WANTED (S.) left waitress 0.00 tip on a $40 tab after she received a Scoutmob discount. If you see this women [sic] in your restaurant tell her to go outside and play hide and go fuck yourself! Yelp that bitch." Within hours, dozens of people "like" the comment and almost as many have "shared" it. Some do venture dissenting opinions, or at least that whatever misdemeanor S. may or may not be guilty of, posting her photo with such a comment is a "disgusting display." The restaurant owner then responds that the person with such an opinion can "go outside and play fuck yourself." As the Facebook situation starts getting out of hand, the restaurant owner reconsiders and decides to remove all comments, replacing them with an apology (of sorts): "After not leaving a tip and the review I lost my lid and made a bad judgment in anger. There is no excuse for my behavior and there is no excuse for not tipping. Sincerely . . ."

It could, of course, end there, but that would go against the human appetite for drama and for talking about drama. So let us now imagine that the story is picked up by a broadsheet, which reports on the negative repercussions for the restaurant in question, particularly its rapidly decreasing ratings on Yelp—the sort of publicity, in short, that would lead the owner to post a more sincere(-looking) apology on Facebook. Something along the lines of

> Dear S., We are truly sorry, it was a bonehead move on our part. But more importantly—it was rude to you and an inappropriate use of social media, which has been a driving force for our business because we can't afford traditional advertising. We rely on word of mouth. Your experience was yours to share and not mine to abuse. This restaurant is my passion and my life. Please give me the opportunity to serve you again at our expense—if not please allow me to fully refund your money on me, Sincerely . . .

This certainly seems to strike the right note of humility. However, just because one person has a change of heart does not mean that everyone else will automatically follow suit. So it should not be surprising to continue to see comments like this one: "Tip your waitresses, assholes. [Restaurant owner], it's the internet. The majority of people railing on you are just being internet trolls and live nowhere near where your restaurant is. . . . If she didn't tip she should've been waterboarded instead." Neither, sadly, should it come as a surprise to find that four people "like" the waterboarding suggestion. But now imagine clicking on that little icon of a thumbs-up next to the number four and discovering that one of the "likes" comes from the self-same restaurant owner.

Perhaps it will not surprise you to learn that this story is not fictional, but recorded as the "Worst Use of Social Media of 2012" (Stratten 2012), involving a real restaurant and real people. It has hopefully dissipated with no real harm to S., and presumably with a lesson learned for the restaurant owner about the mechanics of social media (for instance, that a thumbs-up icon provides a very poor place to hide). But the incident does highlight some of the main themes—both positive and negative—of social media in the food world. First, it is about *conversation*, which is the driving force of social media. New media platforms like blogs, webzines, Facebook, and Twitter have opened up new spaces to talk about food, and virtual communities have blossomed in a very short space of time through sharing recipes and stories across traditional boundaries of place and profession. Many of these communities now also exist in the real world, thanks to events like food blogging conferences, which allow bloggers to meet one another in person. These online platforms are not static repositories of information (even if they can function as archives of information and exchanges some people might wish would go away). One of the defining characteristics of social media in the twenty-first century is "prosumption," or the conflation of consumption and production, which describes the fact that everyone with access to the Internet can potentially contribute to the conversation, and in that way be a producer as well as a consumer of information.

Yet alongside this celebration of the community-building, democratic qualities of the Web and social media are a number of dialogues that betray some anxieties about these new trends. In the domain of restaurant reviewing, for example, professional reviewers increasingly have to defend their livelihoods against the plethora of amateur voices that have the ability to attract an enormous following by virtue of their *non*professionalism—which by some accounts translates to "authenticity," or to the trustworthy voice of the "everyman." Everyone, so the saying goes, is now a critic. This is good news for anyone who wants to join the fray but arguably less so for those who have an interest in safeguarding the professionalism of that practice. So online conversations about who has the right to speak out in a virtual world that permits everyone to have a say are not an uncommon feature of the media landscape. Related here are dialogues around ethics and etiquette when it comes to blogging and to posting comments on blogs and websites, and whether virtual protocols do—or should—differ from those IRL (in real life).

Suggestive of similar concerns are the so-called copyright debates that were topical some years ago, in which signature dishes by celebrity chefs had been "plagiarized" (similarities were picked up through pictures of identical-looking dishes appearing on other restaurant websites). Here the move to copyright was an attempt to uphold a standard of professionalism and exclusivity apparently threatened by the sharing contract of social media. These stories were publicized by the online food forum eGullet.com, which saw it as their responsibility to expose "one of the most significant issues facing the global culinary community today," namely the "ethics in cuisine." The issue of intellectual property rights is moreover not confined to professional kitchens or to celebrity chefs, as amateur cooks and bloggers also routinely confront situations involving the use, and sometimes abuse, of "original" recipes. Finally, there is the perceived threat of digital media to traditional publishing, as the growing availability of (typically free) knowledge and conversations on the Web appears to diminish the demand for (often expensive) print publications. The 2009 closure of *Gourmet* magazine—the "grand dame" of food publications in the United States since its inception in 1941—is a case in point.

The question of anonymity, finally, occupies an intriguing space in the social mediascape, food and otherwise. On the one hand, anonymity has the potential to relieve us of social inhibitions that we may carry in real life: nameless, or pseudonymously, we can say and be anything online (witness the stories of people who invent fantastical versions of themselves in virtual worlds like Second Life and World of Warcraft). Yet, on the other hand, this very potential is also what has made the allowance of anonymity one of the Internet's biggest scourges, as eloquently captured in John Gabriel's 2004 "Greater Internet Dickwad Theory": normal person + anonymity + audience = total dickwad (this is the euphemized version). The number of rude, knee-jerk, offensive, and slanderous comments made incognito all over the Web surely count as good evidence of Gabriel's theory.

Yet, it depends on the audience and, like so much else, on context. When Ruth Reichl was the food critic for the *New York Times* before becoming the editor in chief of *Gourmet* in its final print years, she discovered firsthand (as chronicled in her memoir *Garlic and Sapphires*) how being a nobody was not much fun in restaurants. In 2010, her persona was anonymously "mashed up" (mash-up is the term for combining two technical applications into one) with that of bad-boy celebrity chef Anthony Bourdain to produce the Twitter character @RuthBourdain, who preys on Reichl's actual tweets and translates them into something that fits more comfortably in Bourdain's mouth: essentially cruder, and with more swearing. To @ruthreichl's "Cotton-wrapped city. Visibility zero. One big bowl of super-spicy noodles. Potent broth. Softly poached egg dropped in at the end" (May 24, 2011), for example, @RuthBourdain tweets "Cotton-mouthed city. Visibility zero. Smoked one big bowl of tangerine zest. Potent shit. Dropped some softly poached egg too. Gastrostoned." To Reichl's "Sunshine! Clear sky. The city glistens. Heading out for breakfast on the street. Menu: dumplings, chilied mangoes, spicy tofu" (May 25, 2011), @RuthBourdain gives us "Sunshine! City glistens with Spring's first public urination. Breakfast on the street. Menu: hot dogs, street meat and sidewalk-scraped gum." In 2011, this anonymous character was honored by the James Beard Foundation with the first-ever award in the humor category.

Here, then, anonymity (and a fair amount of crudeness) was rewarded, and @RuthBourdain continues to entertain more than 50,000 followers on a mostly daily basis, including Anthony Bourdain (who is "flattered and disturbed in equal measure"), Ruth Reichl (who finds it "hilarious"), and the soft-spoken Alice Waters of Chez Panisse, who in the spirit of April Fool's Day 2011 issued the truly hilarious tweet: "Yes, It's true. I Am @RuthBourdain." And despite its hardcopy demise, *Gourmet* continues to have a vibrant online presence, including a Facebook page, a YouTube channel, Twitter and Foursquare accounts, and a Gourmet Live app. Also related is an entire new category of literature in the form of "blooks" (books that began as blogs, some of which move on to become big-screen blockbusters, like *Julie & Julia*). These developments suggest that, contrary to the idea of new media replacing or usurping traditional platforms, we are in the midst of a constantly evolving—and constantly challenging, and always fascinating—dialogue of accommodation and adaptation. This book is about that dialogue, which is to say it is about the fast-normalizing trend of relying on social media in the food world. It offers both a historical account of the major changes brought about by the Web and social media and also explores the polarities underlying the various challenges of adaptation, such as exclusivity versus democracy, professionalism versus amateurism, publicity versus privacy, and business versus pleasure (engaging in social media is fun, but it is also rapidly becoming *the* platform for self-promotion and branding, as food bloggers and celebrity chefs have fast discovered).

This is an exciting time to take part in and to document something that changes so rapidly. By no means confined to food, developments in social media, and the possible implications of these developments, are among the liveliest topics of debate today. There is as yet little evidence to support the theory that Google (and the Internet in general) is making us stupid—or indeed the less frequently asked question of whether it might be making us smarter—but there is plenty of emerging research dedicated to discovering what, if anything, the long-term consequences of our ever more-mediated existences might be. As we will see, camps in the food world can be as divided as they are in the scientific community, as new habits challenge our existing models of behavior. Is it, for instance, rude or entirely acceptable to take pictures of your food in a restaurant because you want to blog or tweet it? Some restaurants ban it, while others encourage it. Some diners hate it, while others are too busy tweeting their own pictures to notice. What does it mean, similarly, if cooking becomes more geared to producing a perfect picture for a blog post, rather than the anticipation of sharing a good meal with your friends or family? Some bloggers would say that virtual sharing is no less valuable than anything IRL, while others lament the obsessive compulsion of not being able to relax and let a meal go by undocumented. Are the "time-honored" (which is to say, a few decades old) traditions of restaurant reviewing—repeat visits, accepting no free meals, and so on—worthy of sustained honoring, or has the media landscape shifted so dramatically that the competition between bloggers and "old-school" critics is leveling out and becoming vacuous? Is it OK to blog a recipe you found in a cookbook? What is the difference between being inspired by and adapting a recipe? What is the difference between a blog post and an e-article? Does it matter?

Many of us have opinions on these matters, but most of these questions are as yet unanswered and may well continue to be so until the travails of trial and error bring about some consensus of, if not science or law, then at least best practice when it comes to social media. The chapters that follow document some of the conversations—both popular and academic—that circle around questions of how to behave in this "Information Age." The conversations often emerge out of controversies and therefore bring up issues of how best to respond to virtual conflicts, but plenty concern themselves with the more benign—but ultimately more lucrative—question of how to make the best of an already positive situation. Many of these dialogues take place on social media platforms like Twitter and Facebook, or on blogs, while those that make it to newspaper articles or academic journals are generally inspired by some specific social media exchange. It is for this reason that so many personalities are featured in this book, but it is worth noting that it is not intended as a book of stories about particular people. It is a book of stories about conversations, mostly about food, each of which sheds some light on broader shifts in our cultural—and digital—landscapes.

Chapter 1 gives a brief history of the Web, which is much younger than the Internet. (As its name implies, the Internet is a large interconnected network, whereas the Web is one model for sharing information on that network. Social media are also tools for sharing information, some dependent on the Web, and some on mobile technologies. Although the Web and the Internet are sometimes used synonymously, they are technically distinct.) This chapter also details current numbers of social media users as an index of just how rapidly the Web has grown and fostered connections between millions of people. Some question whether this is a good thing, and particularly in the context of the Web enabling like-minded users to flock together, thereby potentially limiting their exposure to anything that challenges their worldviews. But on the evidence of the food blogging community that is the main subject of this chapter, social media function like a perpetual Thanksgiving dinner: a virtual table for sharing food and for giving thanks for the people seated around it.

Chapter 2 considers another side to this table, which is what happens when its bounty is shared without consent. Here we see examples both of culinary "plagiarism," or the unauthorized reproduction of recipes, and of food writing republished without consent. These cases underline how intellectual property rights are challenged both by the vagaries of legal protection for food and also by apparent confusion between what is publicly visible—which excludes very little on the Web—and what is in the public domain. Reactions to both sets of examples point to the existence of at least some strong *social* norms when it comes to sharing (and not sharing). But these norms, too, are continuously tested by relatively new practices such as taking photographs of food in restaurants, increasingly widespread but still straddling an indeterminate boundary between normal and norm in a virtual context where there are no actual rules.

Chapter 3 sketches an analogy between the "paradox of plenty" in the world of real food—where too much of a good thing can adversely affect our health—and in the realm of food and social media. Here examples range from "foodie-fatigue" (too many people talking about food too much of the time, often in plain service of wasting time) to more potentially damaging scenarios where flippant use of social media can contribute to the spread of misinformation about health and well-being. The Web is, of course, also becoming more and more prominent as a portal for finding and dispensing "good" information about health and well-being, and social media provide tools for campaigning for the same. Much of this advice centers around what not to eat, even as the Web paradoxically offers endless opportunities to look at and to fantasize about everything we are told is "bad" for us.

Chapter 4 takes as its main narrative the current tensions around restaurant criticism. Some of these arise from the proliferation of amateur blogs dedicated to restaurant reviewing and from crowd-sourced review sites like Yelp and Urbanspoon, which pit the single expert against the voices of everyman and of the "wise" (largely anonymous) crowd. Similarly contentious are questions of ethics when it comes to reviewing, and particularly whether providing publicity in exchange for free food is defensible. Notably, despite one common perception that amateur bloggers will do anything for free food, controversies in the latter camp are not exclusive to nonprofessionals. The final part of the chapter focuses on recipe search engines like Google Recipes, which attracted hostility from food bloggers when it was launched thanks to its (programmed) tendency to link to large, established food sites. Contrary to the main concerns around online restaurant reviewing, which sees the established professionalism of that practice under threat, stories around search engines posit bloggers, who are relative newcomers to the public provision of recipes, as the guardians of "real" food.

Chapter 5, finally, details the rise of social media tools—and their users—as becoming ever more important to those in the business of providing food. Noteworthy here is the increased capital of two-way attention as chefs and restaurants discover that one of the most lucrative ways to attract attention to their brands is by giving attention to their consumers, for instance through Twitter and Facebook interactions, and by taking notice of what bloggers and Yelpers are saying about them. The business of food has in this way become more immediate and more "personal." Other examples of this include that fans can now follow the whereabouts of a favorite celebrity chef who "checks in" at restaurants through "geolocation" applications like Foursquare and posts pictures of what he eats on Twitter. But this heightened immediacy and attention also mean that bad publicity can go viral as fast as good publicity, and when that happens, the proverbial wise crowd can quickly turn nasty.

The book concludes with a reminder of some of the challenges—at least the perceived challenges—that have similarly confronted past generations when faced with new technologies. Key among these is the idea of obsolescence: Do digital texts, for instance, render hardcopy books obsolete? More to the point of food, do mobile cooking apps represent a threat to actual cookbooks? There is no evidence (yet) to suggest that this is, or will become, the case. But the future is impossible to predict with absolute certainty, just as many of the phenomena that are unique to social media and that we now already take for granted would have been impossible to imagine just a few decades ago. If that short history teaches us anything, it is that whatever does transpire, we are incredibly good at adapting to it. It should also remind us that although future developments might find us talking about food in virtual spaces we can still not imagine, for as long as we have appetite, we will talk food.

Chapter One

Food for Sharing

Before we get to the food, let us review some numbers that help to describe the social media phenomenon and its phenomenal growth. Facebook, established in 2004, connects more than 800 million users daily (meaning that if it were a country, Facebook would be bigger than the United States). Twitter, established in 2006, connects more than 200 million users. It took three years, two months, and one day to generate the first billion tweets. Now about 1 billion tweets go out every week. In February 2011, Twitter was averaging about half a million new accounts per day. When Michael Jackson died in June 2009, Twitter users set a new record of 456 tweets per second (TPS). By March 2011, the TPS record was 6,396 (@twitter 2011a). In August of that year, news of singer Beyoncé's pregnancy set a new TPS record of close to 9,000 (@twitter 2011b). On New Year's Eve 2011, Japanese tweeters set a new record of 16,197 TPS and crashed the site as a result (Hastings and Fisher 2012). In 1999, there existed about fifty blogs. In 2005, there were more than 30 million, with about 1.6 million blog posts per day (Solove 2007, 21). By the end of 2010, there were more than 150 million blogs on the Internet (Pingdom 2010). There is naturally more to social media than Twitter, Facebook, and blogging, but as designer Angela Nielsen put it on an infographic: "Social Media isn't a fad . . . it's THE way we now communicate with our friend, client, prospect, grandmother, colleague, investor, doctor, realtor, teacher, dietician, veterinarian, grocer, pastor, hairdresser . . ." (Nielsen 2011).

THE WEB: HISTORY AND CRITICISM

Of course, none of this would be possible without the World Wide Web. At a 2007 conference, Kevin Kelly, the founding editor of *Wired* magazine, pointed out that the Web is "less than five thousand days old. . . . This abundance of things that are right before us, sitting in front of our laptop or our desktop . . . this kind of cornucopia of stuff just coming over, never ending, is amazing. And we're not amazed."[1] Taken with some of the numbers he provided—2 million emails per second, 100 billion clicks per day, 55 trillion links (almost equivalent to the number of synapses in our brains), and that at its then-current rate of growth, the Web would exceed humanity in processing power by 2040—it is a fitting reminder of the tremendous size and capability of this new technology and also of the astounding speed at which we have become accustomed to it. Contemplating how unimaginable all of this was a mere decade earlier (including that most of it is free), Kelly suggested that the first lesson of the Web is that we "have to get good at believing in the impossible"—or as he put it in an earlier essay, "if we have learned anything in the past decade, it is the plausibility of the impossible" (Kelly 2005).

There are some things today that might not have seemed impossible in 2007 but that were then still speculative or belonged to an earlier Web generation than the one we find ourselves in today. When Tim Berners-Lee put the first Web page online (which is to say onto the Internet, the system of computer networks that had existed for several decades already) in August 1991, the idea was to create a network—what we now know as the World Wide Web—based on linking computers to one another to facilitate document sharing: an open collective of sorts, of mostly static information. The second phase, also referred to by some as Web 2.0, is characterized by linking information rather than machines, and linking users through that shared information. Web 2.0 is also when we see easier data retrieval through formats like Real Simple Syndication (RSS), which brings content directly to users, and the ability to access the Web from our phones and gaming consoles. Crucially for the development of social media, this phase also has the Internet opening up to accommodate user-generated content like Wikipedia, YouTube, and blogs, including the ability to post comments and customer reviews on retail sites like Amazon. Some Web developers envisage the next generation (known either as Web 3.0, or in Berners-Lee's version, the "Semantic Web") as still being defined by connections between data, rather than people, but with the aim of simplifying everything for the end user. This concept is premised on complete personalization, or the idea that all people who use the Web will have a unique profile based on their personal characteristics (likes, dislikes, friends, location, search history, and so on), which allows the Web, or the so-called "cloud," to provide information uniquely suited to individual contexts. For that to transpire, we, of course, need to make everything about ourselves available to the "machine," as Kevin Kelly calls it. In his summary of this future version of the Web, "total personalization requires total transparency," which mandates Kelly's view that "to share is to gain."

Total personalization might not yet be the norm, but as any of us who pay attention to the ads above Gmail inboxes will have noticed, customized advertising has fast become standard, and Google's Instant Pages feature almost makes it seem like the computer can read our minds (Manjoo 2011a). Similarly possible now is that two people who perform the exact same Google search will receive very different results, as Eli Pariser—who describes himself as an "online organizer and disorganizer"—discovered when he asked two friends to Google "Egypt," and one got directed to the (then ongoing) revolution in Egypt, while the other friend's top hits were travel and vacation links. Pariser uses this example to talk about what he perceives as the danger of "filter bubbles": "Your own personal unique universe of information that you live in online." He concludes that personalization amounts to the "Internet showing what it thinks we want to see, but not necessarily what we need to see." When this happens, he argues, "Instead of a balanced information diet, you can end up surrounded by information junk food" (Pariser 2011), here echoing the "toxic environment" analogy familiar to food scholars as describing the relationship between obesity prevalence and the ubiquity of cheap, "unhealthy" food (figure 1).

Pariser is one among a number of critics of the Web and how it affects us. This is not to say that he (or like-minded critics) advocates switching it off or not using it. Rather, these critics call for a more critical awareness of the way it works, and of the ways in which it may "work" us to our potential disadvantage. At the heart of much of the ongoing debate is the question of attention, which has become our scarcest commodity thanks to the abundance of information at hand. As the economist Herbert Simon theorized several decades ago, "In a world where information is relatively scarce, . . . information is almost always a positive good. In a world where attention is a major scarce resource, information may be an expensive luxury, for it may turn our attention from what is important to what is unimportant" (Simon 1978, 13). Continuing the food analogy, what this means is that while we may have large imaginary appetites, in practice we simply do not have the time, money, or the biological capacity to consume everything available to us. One of the ways to maximize the benefits of living in an attention economy is, then, to become more selective of what we choose to consume, or to do our best to ensure that our information diets are adequately balanced between the important and the unimportant.

Figure 1.1.   Eli Pariser's filter bubble. Courtesy of Eli Pariser.

But the problem that Simon intuited, and which now increasingly concerns media critics like Pariser, is that we are given less choice, or at least that the range of our choices is becoming less visible as our interactions with the "machine" become more customized. Ethan Zuckerman, cyber scholar and director of the MIT Center for Civic Media, uses the word homophily (Latin for "love of the same") to describe the tendency of like-minded people to gather through social media channels: through "friend" recommendations; sites like Facebook encourage similar users to flock together like "birds of a feather," with the result that "we end up in a situation where we don't have as broad a view of the world as we need, and we tend to think that our view is broader than it is" (quoted in de Waal 2010). It is the plausibility of the Web fostering this kind of confirmation bias that is behind Zuckerman's aphorism that "homophily can make you stupid" (quoted in de Waal 2010). That stated, he is quick to point out that there exist competing models, one of which he calls xenophilia ("love of the unknown"), which compels people to seek out new people and information, at least some of which are likely to challenge our existing worldviews. "But xenophilia's hard," he continues. "It's one thing to say to oneself, 'I really should pay attention to matters in Somalia' and another thing to do it. . . . At Berkman [Center for Internet and Society at Harvard University], we've been discussing the problem in terms of broccoli and chocolate—you know you should eat broccoli because it's good for you, but there's just so much tasty chocolate out there!" (Zuckerman 2008).

These are just some of the contributors to wide-ranging conversations about the Web and social media. And just as there is little consensus among media scholars about which generation of the Web we are currently in, a good deal of the dialogue circles around whether we should be worried about where we are heading, or celebrating, or not paying it too much attention either way. In his review of a spate of new books about the Internet, Adam Gopnik describes these three camps as the "Never-Betters," the "Better-Nevers," and the "Ever-Wasers":

> The Never-Betters believe that we're on the brink of a new utopia, where information will be free and democratic, news will be made from the bottom up, love will reign, and cookies will bake themselves. The Better-Nevers think that we would have been better off if the whole thing had never happened, that the world that is coming to an end is superior to the one that is taking its place, and that, at a minimum, books and magazines create private space for minds in ways that twenty-second bursts of information don't. The Ever-Wasers insist that at any moment in modernity something like this is going on, and that a new way of organizing data and connecting users is always thrilling to some and chilling to others—that something like this is going on is exactly what makes it a modern moment. One's hopes rest with the Never-Betters; one's head with the Ever-Wasers; and one's heart? Well, twenty or so books in, one's heart tends to move toward the Better-Nevers, and then bounce back toward someplace that looks more like home. (Gopnik 2011)

Summarizing his own ethos, Gopnik concludes with a prescient reminder—or hope, perhaps—that we are still in charge of what we do with the technology available to us: "Toast, as every breakfaster knows, isn't really about the quality of the bread or how it's sliced or even the toaster. For man cannot live by toast alone. It's all about the butter" (2011). So, while the resolution of these disputes remains to be seen, one trend that is clear is that food references are popular in all camps. This is perhaps fitting, because if there is one area that has been revolutionized by social media, it is in the world of food—or more accurately, in the virtual spaces that accommodate the communication of, dialogues about, and attention to food. Social media do what food does best: they bring people together.

VIRTUAL FOOD(IE) COMMUNITIES

From the founding of Chowhound, one of the first online discussion forums dedicated to food, in 1997 (also the year that the term "weblog" was coined, which would eventually be shortened to "blog"), the Internet has functioned as a powerful generator of virtual food communities, attracting both professionals and amateurs to discuss, to rate, to ask questions, and to find answers.

In 2005, the *Washington Post* reported that *Cooking Light*, one of the top-selling food magazines in the United States, had spawned an "enthusiastic, [sic] community of readers through the message boards on its Web site," some of whom also started gathering in real life for "grassroots" supper clubs (Sagon 2005). While magazines like *Cooking Light* do have "long histories of connecting readers through contests, school and reader-submitted recipes" (Tedeschi 2007), the unique capacity of the Web for connecting people with no geographical proximity is what incentivized leading food sites to generate platforms specifically for social networking, like the "My Epi" section that Epicurious launched in 2007 as one of the first of its kind: "a set of online tools perhaps best characterized as Facebook for foodies," allowing users to "search the virtual recipe boxes of other users, create profile pages for themselves and sift through profiles of other users with whom they may share similar interests" (Tedeschi 2007).

This hardly sounds revolutionary now, although it certainly was less than a decade ago. Surfing the virtual food world today, one would be forgiven for imagining that people had been sharing recipes—and reactions to those recipes—online for decades, so dizzying is the bounty. Some version of the "Facebook for foodies" concept is manifest on practically every top food site, and users are constantly encouraged to extend the conversation to other communities. Find a recipe you enjoy? After you have saved it to your on-site virtual recipe box, you can "like" it on Facebook, tweet it, +1, Digg it, or submit it to Reddit, StumbleUpon, MySpace, or (the aptly named) Delicious—any and all of which add value to the original site by generating the Web traffic crucial to the positive feedback loop of social media: attention from the world inspires attention to the product, which generates more attention from the world, and so on. So it is that a site like Epicurious could in 2011 boast a total of 18 Webby Awards (presented by The International Academy of Digital Arts and Sciences, Webbys are "the leading international award[s] honoring excellence on the Internet including Websites, interactive advertising and online film and video"),[2] the latest two of which were for "Best Food and Beverage Web site," and the "People's Choice Award." Another site notable for Webby recognition is BakeSpace. Launched in 2006 with the motto, "Come for the food. Stay for the conversation," the site is defined as "a grassroots online community where people from around the world gather to share recipes, build new friendships, learn from one another and express their passion for all things food related."[3] BakeSpace has repeatedly been recognized as an official Webby Honoree in the category "Best Social Network" (2007–2010) and in 2011 was an honoree in the "Social Media" category.

There now exist dozens of website collectives in the mold of Epicurious and BakeSpace, but nowhere is the sense of social networking more apparent than in the explosive arena of personal food blogs.[4] Estimated at close to

50,000 in the United States in 2007 (Sylva 2007), food blogs are about virtual camaraderie as much as they are about food. Elise Bauer, host of the multiple award-winning blog Simply Recipes (also listed as one of *Time*'s "50 Coolest Websites 2006" and one of "Eight of the Very Best Food Bloggers" by *Forbes* in 2010), explains the appeal: "Blogging is extremely easy. It doesn't cost anything. There is this whole community aspect, too. It's not just having your own soapbox. It's connecting with other people who have the same passions you do. Food and cooking is about sharing" (quoted in Sylva 2007). Molly Wizenberg, the woman behind the similarly popular and lauded blog Orangette (listed by *The* [UK] *Times* as one of "50 of the world's best food blogs," and winner of the Well Fed Network's "Best Overall Food Blog" in 2005), concurs: "Blogs are like sitting down in the kitchen with someone, only that kitchen is on a computer screen. . . . Most of us who love to cook and eat also love, I think, to talk about cooking and eating, and blogs are an ideal space for that. I can't think of a better way to share my love of food, and to (hopefully) inspire other people to get into the kitchen, too" (quoted in Robinson 2009).

Wizenberg is one of a growing number of food bloggers whose popularity has led to one or more book—or "blook"—deals (two, in Wizenberg's case). While some controversy exists as to the exact definition of a blook (Pierce 2005), it broadly refers to "books based on blogs or websites," as the home of the Blooker Prize (previously the Lulu Blooker Prize, launched in 2006) describes it.[5] On the Blooker panel of judges sits Julie Powell, winner of their first award, and perhaps the best-known food blogger for authoring the Julie/Julia Project, the blog in which she documented cooking her way through Julia Child's *Mastering the Art of French Cooking* over the course of one year (Powell was in competition with another famous blog-based book that year, Brooke Magnanti's *Belle De Jour: The Intimate Adventures of a London Call-Girl*, which one press release humorously translated as "Cooker Beats Hooker to Win Blooker").[6] Powell's blook was published in 2005 as *Julie and Julia: 365 Days, 524 Recipes, 1 Tiny Apartment Kitchen* and later adapted for the big screen in the 2009 film *Julie & Julia*, with Meryl Streep in the role of Julia Child. (The Julie/Julia Project has since been given new life by Lawrence Dai, who describes himself as "a college student with way too much time on my hands," and who decided to spend that time watching the film every day for one year and blogging about the experience on the Lawrence/Julie & Julia Project. We return to Dai's project in chapter 3.)

Taxonomy is a difficult—and often questionable—task, and in the world of food blogging, there is indeed little sense in trying to fit all the output into neat categories. Not all books that began as blogs, for instance, are simply print versions of their digital inspiration (Phipps 2011), and some blogs, similarly, function as digital counterparts to existing print and/or "real-world" culinary profiles. In preparing *The Smitten Kitchen Cookbook*, which grew out of the Smitten Kitchen blog (attracting up to 4 million unique views a month), author Deb Perelman explains that only 10 to 15 percent of recipes from her blog made it into the cookbook, but that she had to put in "the greatest hits or it wouldn't feel like the Smitten Kitchen cookbook" (quoted in Jacob 2011). It is arguably the sense of the personal voice as much as it is the food on display that accounts for the phenomenal success of some bloggers, as is equally apparent in the number of food blogging conference sessions focused on how to cultivate a unique voice—or brand—in such a competitive environment. Here, aspiring bloggers are typically counseled with some variation of "pitch yourself!" as food critic and Life is Lemonade blogger Meridith Ford Goldman put it during the closing keynote address at the Blogher Food '11 conference.[7]

One such well-pitched blogger/writer/cook is David Lebovitz, who began blogging after a long career as a professional baker (he worked as a pastry chef at Chez Panisse for more than a decade). He explains on his blog that it was originally "intended as a place to share recipes and stories [following the publication of his first book, *Room for Dessert*], and in 2004, . . . software which allowed me to post more frequently became available and I turned the site into an official blog."[8] So while the line between what distinguishes a blog from an official website—or a blog post from an article, for that matter (Manjoo 2010)—is likewise tenuous today, styling it as a blog evidently allows for a more "personal" voice, which has certainly been valuable, if not vital, for Lebovitz's continued popularity in an age of social media "friending." As *Publisher's Weekly* in 2009 described his then latest book, *Living the Sweet Life in Paris* (also the tagline of his blog), "Writing with the same cheeky tone that has made his blog one of the most popular food sites on the Internet, Lebovitz presents an eclectic collection of vignettes illustrating his experiences living as an expatriate in Paris."[9] Another famous Parisian, finally, who is as well known for her now-several books as for her award-winning blog, Chocolate and Zucchini, is Clotilde Dusoulier. Reviewing her first cookbook, a writer for the *New York Times* summarized what could be the ethos of food blogging: "Dusoulier is the Parisian friend we all wish we had" (Crapanzano 2007).

Fantasy friends are not a new phenomenon. Social scientists Donald Horton and Richard Wohl coined the term "para-social interaction" in the 1950s to describe the particular (and peculiar) kind of relationship that exists between one person and a score of followers—typically between celebrities and fans, and then most obviously generated through the mass impact of television.[10] Communications professor Joshua Meyrowitz summarizes:

> They [Horton and Wohl] argue that although the relationship is mediated, it psychologically resembles face-face interaction. Viewers come to feel they "know" the people they "meet" on television in the same way they know their

friends and associates. In fact, many viewers begin to believe that they know and understand a performer better than all the other viewers do. Paradoxically, the para-social performer is able to establish "intimacy with millions." (Meyrowitz 1985, 119)

Blogs—now increasingly in tandem with companion social media platforms like Twitter and Facebook, which help to generate an even greater sense of immediacy and proximity—are ideal platforms for engendering this kind of relationship, thanks both to the personalized nature of much of their content and to readers' ability to comment on site. Although it could be argued that the interactive allowances of social media change the one-way model of this relationship as it manifests through television viewing, equally plausible is the possibility that new media simply intensify the experience precisely because of the liveliness of exchange. In other words, although regular readers and commenters may also become "known" to bloggers, until the unguaranteed event that they actually meet in person, the single blogger continues to foster intimacy, if not with millions, then with hundreds or thousands.

Food blogging, moreover, has the potential to become even more intimate, dealing as it does with something so mundane and necessary, and at the same time so metaphorically loaded. As Molly Wizenberg pointed out, most of us love to eat, and we also love to tell stories through food. Consider the account of one reader (and blogger):

> When you read a writer's words and see what their cameras capture every day, their lives become an integrated, regular part of your own. If you're like me, you remember when Smitten Kitchen announced her pregnancy with a recipe for cream cheese–covered cinnamon buns and an adorable reference to the other bun in the oven. Maybe, like me, you got a little teary eyed and hung in there when The Wednesday Chef revealed, with a forlorn can of baked beans and a broken heart, that she wasn't ready to start cooking again so soon after the end of a major relationship. And you might have gasped with glee when Orangette told us that she got engaged over champagne and chocolate truffles to the young man for whom she'd baked orange-nutmeg muffins. (Suthivarakom 2011a)

There can be little doubt that the majority of food bloggers—or at least those who are rewarded with enough attention to make a success of their activities, which perhaps includes the knowledge that they are adding value to other people's lives—would consider themselves what Gopnik calls Never-Betters when it comes to the Web and its impact on our lives. Certainly this is the case for bloggers like Shauna James Ahern, aka Gluten-Free Girl, who began a blog of that name after having celiac disease diagnosed. Her blog (also regularly hailed as one of the "best," and its follow-up book the subject of glowing reviews) has grown into an "online coffeehouse for people who share the digestive condition. . . . But don't expect a lot of moaning and groaning and symptom-swapping. In fact, it's easy to forget that the blog revolves around gluten-free eating because there are so many gloriously decadent food photos. And because Ahern is determined to celebrate what she can eat—not what she can't" (Lynch 2010).

Stories like Gluten-Free Girl's exemplify the scenario in which sharing fosters community not only for the sake of vicarious engagement, but also as a potential service for those of her readers who share her condition and who may find inspiration to, like her, celebrate what they can eat rather than lament what they cannot enjoy. That said, it is likely the case that the communities that grow out of the combined attention to the food blogosphere—gluten-free and not—are fueled in equal measure by taking vicarious pleasure in food and taking inspiration to enjoy some of that food by re-creating it (or something based on it) in real life—although the sheer abundance of what is available precludes every inspiration from coming to fruition. This is probably not so different from the dozens of cookbooks many of us have on our shelves containing countless fantasy meals that we will never get around to cooking, except that the personal element of many blogs puts on display people's lives as much as the food that they cook.

PIONEER WOMEN: BIRDS OF A FEATHER

One blogger whose life features as prominently as (if not more than) her food and who has attracted a phenomenal following is Ree Drummond, or The Pioneer Woman. Drummond's blog chronicles her life on a cattle ranch with her husband, aka Marlboro Man, her four children, and their dog, Charlie (who is the subject of a children's book, *Charlie the Ranch Dog*). Drummond describes herself on the blog as "a desperate housewife. I live in the country. I channel Lucille Ball, Vivien Leigh, and Ethel Merman. Welcome to my frontier!"[11] Technically, it is a frontier that challenges any distinction that may exist between a blog and a website, and also between a general blog and a *food* blog, because in appearance it is a professionally constructed portal into the many different aspects of Drummond's life. In addition to her "Cooking" section (featuring "P.W." recipes), and a "Tasty Kitchen Blog" (featuring blog posts and recipes from registered members), the site has sections dedicated to homeschooling tips, photography, home and garden, entertainment (including favorite movies), and "Confessions," which features stories and pictures about her life and family. Drummond regularly hosts competitions or quizzes on the site, in which she (Oprah style) gives away some her favorite things: KitchenAid appliances, Apple store and Amazon gift vouchers, and so on. As for the details of daily life on that frontier, a *New Yorker* profile explains:

Drummond doesn't discuss politics or engage in cultural criticism; she doesn't even gossip. Whole continents of contemporary worry go unmentioned: this is a universe free from credit-card debt, toxins, "work-life balance," and marital strife. The blog provides an escape from the viperous forces elsewhere on the Internet. Depending on your circumstance and your disposition, the relentless good cheer can seem either admirable or annoying. . . . Drummond makes an average life look heroic. (Fortini 2011)

As we will see shortly, Drummond does annoy some people (very much), but she also attracts enough positive attention to account for generating "solidly one million" dollars in ad revenue in 2010, for winning a number of blog awards over the years (notably "Best Food Blog" in 2008 and "Weblog of the Year" in 2009), for her cookbook hitting number one on the *New York Times* best-seller list, for her memoir being optioned by Sony Pictures (with Reese Witherspoon in the lead role), and for Drummond to be given her own show on the Food Network.

The focus on what Drummond does *not* provide is interesting for what it reveals about what we expect of so-called food bloggers (and perhaps of bloggers in general). Compared with other high-profile food media personalities—consider the likes of television cooks Giada de Laurentiis, Sandra Lee, and Nigella Lawson—Drummond is not alone in providing an "escape" from the drudgeries, irritations, and challenges of an "average" everyday life. It is true that these (television) figures frame many of their recipes as "easy" solutions to precisely those unglamorous circumstances, but like Drummond's recipes—and like Drummond herself—they are typically presented in a way that promises the potential of effortless glamour. Yet television has always operated on a level of artifice. Historically (until the advent of reality TV at least), it is a medium of performance, not disclosure. The Web, conversely, is about revelation and discovery. It is, in perception at least, about making "real" connections.

These are the kinds of connections that can mobilize the food blogging community to dedicate a day to baking a peanut butter pie to share with someone they love at the request of Jennifer Perillo, a fellow blogger who had recently lost her husband, and who invited people—some actual friends, mostly strangers—to help her to celebrate her husband's life: a cooperative spirit in the face of a tragic, and very real, situation.[12] The description of Drummond's blog as an "escape," in contrast, suggests a degree of affectation, if not outright deception. The "average" life made to look "heroic" might very well be a large part of Drummond's appeal. It can be inspirational and aspirational, much like Nigella Lawson's television persona represents an idealized—which is to say unrealistic—version of the so-called work-life balance. Yet Drummond's heroic frontier life has earned her the scorn of at least three other bloggers, whose regular posts calling her out as a fake, and her fans as duped, are celebrated in the dozens (sometimes hundreds) of comments on their respective blogs. The Pioneer Woman Sux blog, subtitled "Plowing through her bullshit . . . one deceit at a time," takes as its mission fulfilling what is an apparent Web tradition:

> All the cool kids get a Sux. Rachel [sic] Ray, Survivor, you name it and they've got one. So you knew that sooner or later PW would get one too. We'll explore over here. We'll dissect her content to find the heart of it. We'll poke fun and we'll expose just how fucking stupid all her sheeple followers are. [13]

Apart from copious ridiculing in the name of said tradition, The Pioneer Woman Sux seems fueled by the idea—understood as a problem—that "Ree Drummond no longer exists. Readers are now presented with the sanitized and trademarked Pioneer Woman. A brand. Nothing more, nothing less" (PWSux 2011a). It is this perceived condescension of being "unreal" that similarly provides fodder for The Marlboro Woman (dedicated to "Keepin' the Pioneer Woman Real!"),[14] and Pie Near Woman, a blog that satirizes the Pioneer Woman with picture stories featuring plastic dolls, typically in sexually provocative positions.

The question of making the personal public, and of whether it ought to remain private, is one of the topics that trouble some media scholars. These debates largely revolve around how much control we have over our private data (Solove 2007, 2011; Carr 2010a; Harper 2010; Lohr 2010), but the kind of voluntary publication of the personal and/or private that blogs (and Facebook and Twitter) allow is similarly worrying to critics like Andrew Keen, who maintains, pessimistically, that "we are becoming the WikiLeakers of our lives." Keen cites two American psychologists who have described this "contemporary mania with self-expression" as "the narcissism epidemic": "a self-promotional madness driven . . . by our need to broadcast our uniqueness to the world" (Keen 2011). The example of the Pioneer Woman, and more particularly of her detractors, is a curious reminder that seldom in deliberations about online privacy and what we choose to communicate to the world is the truth-value of those disclosures questioned (excepting scare stories like the ones involving pedophiles posing as someone else, that is). Rarely when we read a story about someone's life in a blog do we stop to wonder whether that story, unique or not, is in fact true.

This is not to join her hecklers in suggesting that the Pioneer Woman tells lies on her blog. It is, rather, to point out how much we generally do take at face value, because the social mechanics of the Web encourage confidence (understood here both as making virtual confidants of strangers, and as having confidence in those connections as "real"), even as much of what many of us do online is patently some form of performance. Author Peggy Orenstein put it well in her account of coming to Twitter for the first time, where she initially experienced an unexpected candor: "Distilling my personality provided surprising focus, making me feel stripped to my essence." Later she realized that what she decided to tweet "was not really about my own impressions: it was how I imagined—and wanted—others to react to them. . . . How much, I began to wonder, was I shaping my Twitter feed, and how much was Twitter shaping me?" (Orenstein 2010).

It is possible that this self-consciousness is related to the divide between so-called digital natives and immigrants, the former having grown up with information technology, while the latter have had to unlearn "old" ways while adapting to new ones (Prensky 2001).[15] It is also possible that as a writer, Orenstein is more sensitive to the fact that whenever we present a mediated version of ourselves to others, be it on paper, in a photograph, on a blog, or through Twitter, it is always a *representation*, which means we always have the option to pose as we would like to be seen, rather than as we actually are. Nonetheless, a narrowing of the gap between digital immigrants and natives is certainly a step toward one future version of the Web that has us all losing our self-consciousness about how we conduct ourselves online. As Oliver Burkeman put it after attending the 2011 South by Southwest festival of film, music, and technology, "If Web 2.0 was the moment when the collaborative promise of the internet seemed finally to be realised—with ordinary users creating instead of just consuming, on sites from Flickr to Facebook to Wikipedia—Web 3.0 is the moment they forget they're doing it" (Burkeman 2011).

Whether this has—or ever will—fully come to pass, and what the implications of that eventuality may be, are larger technical and philosophical questions than we can concern ourselves with here. Yet Burkeman's description of Web 3.0 does give some weight to computer scientist and virtual reality pioneer Jaron Lanier's chilling claim that "we tinker with your philosophy by direct manipulation of your cognitive experience, not indirectly, through argument" (Lanier 2010, 6). If it is true that our "philosophies"— which is to say the values we attach to truth and knowledge, and how they inform how we interact and reason with the world—are manipulated by the technologies we use, this could account for one fundamental irony in the existence of projects like The Pioneer Woman Sux, The Marlboro Woman, and Pie Near Woman: anonymously dedicated to outing the "truth" by dissecting virtually every move the Pioneer Woman makes, these are no less constructs than their target, and no less branded than the brand they take issue with.

"Prosumption," or the license to produce media as well as to consume it, is one of the features that do make the Web amazing, to borrow Kevin Kelly's term. It is an amazing feature because producing includes the possibility of contributing in a meaningful way and of adding value to a dialogue previously dominated by the "powers that be." Now, if we like something, we can say so, and hope that our input will contribute to maintaining, or to improving, that thing that we like. If we see, or read, or experience something that we do not like, we are also free to say so on numerous platforms. And if we dislike it enough to commit to the time and energy it takes to maintaining a regular blog dedicated to expressing that dislike, then we are likewise free to do so. As PWSux put it in one post responding to the charge of being a cyberbully, a troll, a griefer, or the host of a hate-site, [16] "For the record, I don't 'hate' Ree Drummond. I don't want to 'take her down' or 'prove anything' or 'convince anyone' or any of the things I've seen as speculation for this site. Please. Get over it. I'm posting my opinions on my own damn site. Period" (2011b). But like the number of anonymous comments littering the Web that are both likely to be nastier than if they were signed, or if someone had taken the time to sit down and put pen to paper (Dalrymple 2010), and also to miss their potential mark because of that, it is worth thinking about what the use value of these pseudonymous blogs may be, and if they even exist outside of the "narcissism epidemic" that they apparently protest.

The point here is not to single out the Pioneer Woman's dissenters for particular scorn or scrutiny either. But they and the communities they foster are good, if inadvertent, examples of homophily and filter bubbles at work and of the questionable qualities of those phenomena in an attention economy. They are certainly entertaining to read (and Pie Near Woman deserves special mention for creativity with dolls), but if you stop to consider the amount of dedication required to be truly parasitic on someone else's prolific output, and combine that with the likelihood that that person is likely not to pay it much attention anyway—or at least whose public profile prevents any direct engagement, and whose continued success probably also curbs the need for such engagement—what remains is a community of cynics who echo and feed off each other's shared gripes: birds of a ruffled feather, as it were. Where there is engagement with the "outside," meaning in this case those of Drummond's fans or allies who venture to challenge any of these bloggers, they are quickly derided as one of the ("fucking stupid") "sheeple."

As the "sux" tradition demonstrates, Ree Drummond is by no means a lone target in the virtual world. And neither is every dissenting voice an angry, a nasty, or an anonymous voice. Mathematics PhD candidate Adam Merberg's blog, Say What, Michael Pollan?, for instance, takes that writer as its subject: "Much as I appreciate what Michael Pollan has done to raise awareness about food-related issues," Merberg writes, "I'm sometimes frustrated by things he says or writes that seem slanted or even incorrect. This blog is an attempt to encourage Pollan to check facts and think through arguments more carefully." [17] But the louder choir in the cyber world of food is made up of consenting voices that take obvious pleasure in sharing and often in honoring the source of their inspiration. The blog, Not Too Much—Mostly Plants? took inspiration from Pollan's now-famous dictum to eat whole foods for a year. The author of Not Quite Nigella (who also landed a publishing deal for a cookblook of the same name) tells us that, "Yes, Nigella Lawson has visited . . . , and loves the name."[18] And from the host of French Laundry At Home, in her last post on that blog (before moving onto Alinea At Home), titled "Thank You" (the first thanks of which went to Thomas Keller):

> I've been incredibly lucky these past two years. I've been able to meet some people I've admired from afar, and I've been given some amazing opportunities that continue to open doors I never could've imagined. . . . It makes me happy to know there are so many busy, hardworking people out there—home cooks just like me—who want to stretch their wings and spend all day cooking something special . . . . I love that we've been able to connect through this and other blogs. (Blymire 2008)

(For the lucky ones, there is more than "just" connection to be found: Wizenberg famously met her husband through her blog, and for those without blogs, foodie dating sites like Food Lovers Passions and Spoondate are on the rise.)

So perhaps it is not entirely true that we are not amazed by the Web. I would venture, though, that when we are amazed, it is at where we find ourselves, rather than how we got there. Like arriving at the Grand Canyon and being awestruck by its splendor, but forgetting to marvel at the technology that transported us there. Then again, paying less attention to the mechanics of transport and more to our surroundings is exactly in line with what the author of the Web had in mind: "Its [sic] not the Social Network *Sites* that are interesting—it is the Social Network itself. The Social Graph. The way I am connected, not the way my Web pages are connected. . . . It is about getting excited about connections, rather than nervous" (Berners-Lee 2007, emphasis in the original). In the virtual food world at least there can be no questioning that excitement trumps nervousness—even if a few feathers do get ruffled along the way.

NOTES

1. Kelly was speaking at the annual Entertainment Gathering (EG) Conference ("the premiere gathering of and for innovators in media, technology, entertainment and education"). A video of the talk is available at http://www.youtube.com/watch?v=yDYCf4ONh5M (accessed March 2, 2011).

2. http://www.webbyawards.com/about/ (accessed October 3, 2011).

3. http://www.bakespace.com/ (accessed September 20, 2011).

4. For a timeline featuring the most popular food blogs and aggregated sites, see Suthivarakom 2011b. Bridging the divide between collectives and individual blogs are online groups like the Daring Bakers and Charcutepalooza. Although focused on different outcomes (baking and charcuterie, respectively), they share a model based on members individually blogging about collective challenges.

5. http://www.blookerprize.com/ (accessed June 3, 2011).

6. http://www.prweb.com/releases/2006/04/prweb367086.htm (accessed June 3, 2011).

7. http://www.blogher.com/blogher-food-11-closing-keynote-liveblog?wrap=node/ 364836/virtual-conference/posts (accessed September 15, 2011).

8. http://www.davidlebovitz.com/about/ (accessed July 10, 2011).

9. http://www.publishersweekly.com/978-0-7679-2888-5 (accessed August 5, 2011).

10. On para-social interaction as a feature of food television, see Collins 2009, 176.

11. http://thepioneerwoman.com/ (accessed July 10, 2011).

12. In August 2011, Perillo, host of the blog In Jennie's Kitchen, lost her husband to a sudden heart attack. In a post titled "for mikey," she wrote: "For those asking what they can do to help with my healing process, make a peanut butter pie this Friday and share it with someone you love. Then hug them like there's no tomorrow because today is the only guarantee we can count on" (Perillo 2011). The request was widely tweeted (and retweeted) by the food blogging community, and a Facebook page was constructed for the public event "Peanut Butter Pie Friday for Mikey and Jennifer Perillo." As of that Friday (August 12, 2011), the event had 364 members "attending," many of whom had posted pictures of their pies and written tributes to a man they had never met. For the next few days, the first several pages of Tastespotting (a site dedicated to showcasing pictures of food submitted by users around the world) were dominated by pictures of peanut butter pies "for Mikey." Perillo's plight also became the subject of the Twitter hashtag #afundforjennie, which in turn inspired the blogger-based charity Bloggers Without Borders (BWoB). In October 2011, BWoB announced that the total amount raised for Perillo's family was $76,430.50, which would be transferred into education savings accounts for her two daughters (Keet 2011).

13. http://www.thepioneerwomansux.com/about/ (accessed July 10, 2011).

14. http://themarlborowoman.com/ (accessed June 3, 2011).

15. Prensky (2001) characterizes digital immigrants as typically retaining a "foot in the past" or an accent, much like people who learn a new language: "The 'digital immigrant accent' can be seen in such things as turning to the Internet for information second rather than first, or in reading the manual for a program rather than assuming that the program itself will teach us to use it." Prensky's theory is not without contention, as several studies claim to debunk the existence of the divide he proposed. See, for example, Bennett, Maton, and Kervin 2008; and Jones and Czerniewicz 2010.

16. Cyberbullying, trolling, griefing, and hosting hate-sites variously describe online behavior intended to provoke, embarrass, or discredit someone or to destabilize a virtual environment such as a discussion forum or a game. For the post in question, see Kellog 2011.

17. http://saywhatmichaelpollan.wordpress.com/ (accessed March 10, 2011).

18. http://www.notquitenigella.com/2007/07/15/about/ (accessed November 10, 2010).

Chapter Two

Food Not for Sharing

Sharing recipes for the purposes of re-creation, adaptation, and inspiration is one of the conversational strands that animate the social media food network. But these forms of imitation also sometimes straddle a fine line between flattery and theft, where questions of intellectual property rights sketch a virtual—if not yet legal—boundary around food clearly not meant for unrestricted sharing. In the professional food community, one of the first publicized cases began in 2006, when the eGullet Society for Culinary Arts and Letters posted a series of photographs taken from the website of Interlude, a restaurant in Australia, alongside pictures of almost-identical dishes from two well-known US restaurants: Grant Achatz's Alinea, and Wylie Dufresne's WD-50. The first similarities (between Interlude and WD-50, and also José Andrés's Washington restaurant, Minibar) had been noted by eGullet member and WD-50 pastry chef Sam Mason, after which other members pointed to similarities with Alinea, now "suggesting a substantial pattern of duplication" (eGullet 2006a).

Partly motivated by Interlude (here, the offending party) having removed the images from their website following their ostensible outing, the eGullet staff published the pictures for comparison with a note emphasizing journalistic integrity and professional ethics:

The eGullet Society doesn't have an official position on this matter, but it's appropriate to publish the following for two reasons. First, by presumably removing the photographs from its website, Interlude has made examination of the evidence impossible, unless we bring these photos to light in a journalistic context. Second, we believe the Interlude controversy is not a simple matter of a lone Australian restaurant copying a few dishes from halfway around the world. Rather, it's one of the most significant issues facing the global community today. The eGullet Society and its membership, including most of the world's foremost avant-garde chefs as well as a broad range of consumers and commentators, is a natural nexus for discussion of those issues. Of course, it is our hope that these discussions will influence the understanding of ethics in cuisine, and perhaps worldwide policy in such matters. (eGullet 2006a)

The topic unsurprisingly generated hundreds of responses ranging across the ethical, social, legal, economic, and artistic implications of using other people's ideas and the urgency of being credited for one's own.

CULINARY PLAGIARISM: LEGAL PROTECTION VS. SOCIAL NORMS

Had the eGullet discussion been confined to literature, or even to written recipes (more about which shortly), questions of plagiarism and intellectual property rights would have been fairly straightforward. But food is more complicated, not least because competence in professional cooking has been—at least since Escoffier codified (and lightened) haute cuisine in his 1903 *Le Guide Culinaire*—measured by the exact reproduction of classic dishes. Even nonprofessionally, borrowing, copying, and adapting are the hallmarks of food in virtually every culinary tradition. As James Beard said of "American" food, "There really are no recipes, only millions of variations sparked by somebody's imagination and desire to be a little bit creative and different. American cooking is built . . . on variations of old recipes from around the world" (quoted in Jones 1990, 240).

Of course the Interlude controversy was not about adaptation but what appeared to be direct duplication of other chefs' creative flourishes on the plate. It was, according to some, a case of stealing someone else's art and presenting it as your own—which would likewise have been an obvious case of theft in the art world. But the status of food as art is less straightforward.[1] For one thing, and unlike most other artifacts, food is made to be consumed. It represents an event, not a thing. One *Guardian* journalist aptly described the trend of "arty" food in her report of the final meal at the famed El Bulli restaurant: "It's like going to an exhibition in which you demonstrated your appreciation by kicking the art off the walls" (Williams 2011). In her legal note on "How to Copyright a Cake" ("an original proposal for extending copyright protection to food"), Malla Pollack also suggests that the range of senses involved in food make it a separate art. Food contains elements of color and form, as do painting and sculpture. Food also includes aromas, tastes, and textures. If food is an art form, it is a new category. . . . [W]hile food may not have been so considered in the eighteenth century, it is so considered now, at least by an epicurean segment of the population. (Pollack 1991, 7)

It is, moreover, this "epicurean" group—to which the eGullet community unquestionably belongs—that would likely be the first to point out that understanding food as art really means acknowledging the chef as an artist, and where appropriate, as an original creator. As Alinea's co-owner Nick Kokonas reported overhearing in the restaurant in response to the pictures, "The thing that bothers me the most, is that if a diner went to Interlude first and then dined at Alinea, that diner would think *we* were copying *him*" ("nick.kokonas," in eGullet 2006, emphases in the original).

"Cooking is the oldest of all arts," wrote Brillat-Savarin in 1852 (1970, 242). This quote also prefaces the article "On the Legal Consequences of Sauces," in which law professor Christopher Buccafusco examines available legal recourses, or the copyrightability of recipes, in the specific context of the Interlude case. So while Pollack is not entirely accurate in saying that food has not been considered art until very recently, both she and Buccafusco draw attention to the complications arising from legal perspectives on the "art" of cooking, and how these implicate both the status of chefs—who were not recognized as professionals by the US Department of Labor until the 1970s (Pollack, 41; Kamp 2006, 10)—and recipes, which span a juridical grey zone between the text and its execution. The problem with legally protecting recipes, simply put, lies somewhere between authorship and performance.

Buccafusco outlines two cases to have reached the US appellate court, one of which involved a lawsuit against Godiva Chocolatier in 1998 for using an unpublished truffle recipe. The court was hostile to the idea of copyrighting recipes, concluding that the "identification of ingredients necessary for the preparation of food is a statement of facts. There is no expressive element deserving copyright protection in each listing" (quoted in Buccafusco 2007, 1129). It is this "expressive" element that is required for a culinary work to be legally recognized as artistic expression. At the time of the Interlude controversy, the official stipulation of the US Copyright Office read as follows:

Mere listings of ingredients in recipes, formulas, compounds or prescriptions are not subject to copyright protection. However, where a recipe or formula is accompanied by substantial literary expression in the form of an explanation or directions, or when there is a combination of recipes, as in a cookbook, there may be basis for copyright protection. . . . Copyright protects only the particular manner of an author's expression in literary, artistic, or musical form. Copyright protection does not extend to names, titles, short phrases, ideas, systems, or methods. (Copyright 2006)

This provision has since been amended to remove the last two quoted sentences, and to add the clause that "only original works of authorship are protected by copyright. 'Original' means that an author produced a work by his or her own intellectual effort instead of copying it from an existing work." So, *original* recipes accompanied by *original* textual narrative are copyrightable. But any existing dish, like apple pie, which is not "original to the author" is not (Buccafusco 2007, 1127). Apple pie, in the eyes of the law, is common property, regardless of its variations.[2]

The legal lacuna that problematized the Interlude controversy, focused as it was on the performance rather than the text of a recipe, is in the final 2006 proviso that copyright "protects only the particular manner of an author's expression in . . . artistic . . . form" but does not cover "ideas, systems, or methods." Were cooking recognized by the law as "artistic," the idea behind a dish, as well as its method—that is, the process of cooking it—would naturally be the main elements of that author's expression. "The important question," says Buccafusco, "is whether a dish, as embodied in a recipe, constitutes a protectable work of authorship" (1128, n40). As both he and Pollack demonstrate, existing legal rhetoric evidently provides no simple answer to that question—or rather, the straightforward-looking Copyright Act does not take account of the potential complexities of individual cases.

But more interesting than navigating the intricacies of the law (a task best left to professionals in that field) is the impetus behind motivations for copyrighting food in the first place, and particularly in a culture increasingly defined by access and sharing. According to Pollack, it is a measure that will encourage *more* sharing and will also eventually benefit the public:

> The current lack of legal protection for culinary creations encourages a refusal to share recipes. . . . Copyright protection for food items will encourage chefs to create and share original food items. As with all copyright protection, the ultimate beneficiary will be the public. Chefs will create more; their creations will not only be available for immediate use but will eventually enter the public domain. (Pollack 1991, 3)

This sort of consideration presumably answers questions like the one posed by a respondent on the eGullet forum: "In reality, who cares if a restaurant in Melbourne offers up a dish from a restaurant in New York, and pretends it's their own? Is it really going to matter ten years from now? 5? 1? In a month? If you do it well, and your own customers appreciate it, isn't that what's important?" ("saltshaker," in eGullet 2006a).

Clearly the experience of the moment is not all that is important for those involved. Just a few months after the Interlude controversy, another one emerged involving the supposed plagiarism of dishes from Minibar by a chef—a former employee at Minibar—at the Tapas Molecular Bar in Tokyo. Claiming that his inventions had been used without his permission, Minibar chef-owner José Andrés motivated either for the payment of a license fee or for the dishes to be removed from the Tokyo menu (McLaughlin 2006). Similarly discussed on eGullet, now under the heading "Further Tales of Culinary Plagiarism," the overwhelming response was not about legalities, but about credit. "Just to be clear on the locus of plagiarism," wrote "Fat Guy" Steve Shaw, eGullet's executive director, "If the chef had done the lobster dish with lobster—exactly the same—and said 'This is a dish made at José Andrés's Minibar in Washington, DC, USA,' it would not have been plagiarism" (eGullet 2006b). There is little to argue about here (except perhaps the last comment on that particular forum, which asked, "What if the one who plagiarizes actually does the dish better?"). But that intellectual or artistic credit is largely rhetorical compared to financial credit is also well illustrated by the very real legal steps taken to protect original culinary creations.

Homaro Cantu, executive chef and founder of Moto restaurant and operator of Cantu Designs in Chicago, provides one good example of successful legal protection. At the forefront of the avant-garde chef community (to which all the suspected plagiarists and plagiarized incidentally belong), Cantu's inventions include novelties like edible paper: diners at his restaurant are expected to eat the menu after ordering from it, and after dinner, to eat the fortune inside the cookie (Shriver 2005). Food writer (and now the restaurant critic for the *New York Times*) Pete Wells's encounter with Cantu, as chronicled in his article on the "New Era of the Recipe Burglar" (2006), was via a small piece of flavored, edible paper imprinted with a picture of candy cotton. More pioneering than the paper, and what Wells called its "truly historic feature," was "the legal notice printed beneath the cotton candy image: 'Confidential Property of and © H. Cantu. Patent Pending. No further use or disclosure is permitted without prior approval of H. Cantu.'" Although that patent was pending, Cantu had, at the time of Wells's writing, twelve patents under way, and the revolutionary potential of the paper included the chef's idea to collaborate with the Red Cross to use it as a form of "lightweight famine relief," provided he could discover how to print nutrients as well as flavors. (NASA had also expressed interest in the new technology "as a way of printing an apple that you can hold in your hand and take to Mars," Cantu explained. "We have a machine that lets you push a button and out comes a picture of an apple. What we don't know how to do yet is to make it three dimensional—how do we make an apple?")

Cantu is also a member of eGullet (under the handle "inventolux"), and his contribution to the "plagiarism" question echoes Pollack's suggestion that copyrighting ultimately serves the interests of the public: "Licencing [sic][3] enables someone to recieve [sic] compensation for their ideas. . . . The whole point of me explaining the broadness of this printed food is to get chefs to think that maybe one of their ideas can solve a massive problem. They should be rewarded for it" (eGullet 2006a). This invocation of credit—be it intellectual, artistic, or financial—where credit is due is unquestionable, and particularly in the case of something with potentially far-reaching benefits beyond the avant-garde chef community. But it is also a curiosity of the twenty-first century that recipe sharing should be circumscribed by legal protection and secrecy (as Wells notes, "Copyrighting recipes may be the most radical idea to hit the food world since the invention of the menu"). Consider the man behind the paper that could alleviate famine:

> When you rely on your intellectual property for income, you suddenly become Bill Gates, building walls around your inventions to keep thieves away. Cantu requires almost everyone who enters his kitchen to sign a four-page nondisclosure agreement. He says he runs background checks on some potential cooks to make sure they're culinary school graduates and not corporate spies, and he uses caller ID just in case that party of two looking for a table next Thursday night is phoning from Burger King headquarters. Cantu says his closed-door policy mainly applies to big business. He's generally happy to talk techniques with fellow chefs. Sometimes, though, even they can't be trusted. (Wells 2006)

Whether it is inspired by suspicion or genuine untrustworthiness, such an environment is telling of some of the tensions that run counter to accessibility as a central feature of global communications in general, and of the virtual food world in particular. One manifestation of these tensions is a progressive narrowing of the line between sharing and stealing. Also, while Wells's analogy may be extreme—there can only be one Bill Gates, after all—Cantu's efforts to safeguard ownership of his ideas also give the lie to any rhetoric in service of the public.

There is no question here of the alleged right or wrong of seeking legal protection for intellectual property, or expecting rightful acknowledgment from peers. And although plagiarism is not a legal issue per se, it is certainly not new: from the Latin *plagiarus* (kidnapper), it described slave- and word-thievery in Roman times (Howard 1995, 790). Escoffier himself is said to have "complained that while artists, writers, musicians and inventors were protected by law, the chef had absolutely no redress for plagiary of his work" (Mennell 1985, 162). Rather, the examples of Cantu and the subjects of the eGullet debates are useful for highlighting a less talked-about aspect of media in a so-called globalized world, where the discursive elimination of boundaries is challenged by an apparent threat of commonality. As the world opens up to a sea of competition from professionals and amateurs alike, chefs distinguish themselves from the crowd by becoming innovators or artists, and by producing creations rather than mere recipes.

This is obviously wonderful news for those diners who delight in having their senses and taste buds seduced by ever more-adventurous combinations and presentations (and who have the financial means to do so). But this increasingly specialized behavior also serves to separate this avant-garde community—Buccafusco calls them the "gastronomic cognoscenti" (2007, 1155)—ever more emphatically from the general public, their supposed beneficiary. For those like Cantu who have secured legal protection, the fact that laws regarding intellectual property are in constant flux and that legal rhetoric is largely incomprehensible to the general public only add to this effect. That said, ignorance does not have to be a deterrent: while we may not understand the specific workings of the law, the familiarity of symbols like ™ (trademarked), © (copyright), and ® (registered trademark) can exert a strong appeal by promising safety and uniqueness. When it comes to patents, attorney and law professor Eugene Quinn explains:

> Enforcing patent rights can be expensive, and in many circumstances I suspect a recipe patent or food product patent would be rather narrow and afford little real protection. Nevertheless, one important reason to obtain a patent is for advertising. Once a patent is applied for you can use in advertising the coveted term "patent pending." If a patent issues you can also advertise "try my patented recipe." The public at large knows very little about patent law, but most recognize that to get a patent means something special (i.e., that is has somehow been anointed by the federal government). (Quinn 1999–2007)

Producing something "special" is vital to a market saturated with endless variations of what is very often really one product (need BBQ sauce? You can choose between those branded by Paula Deen, Guy Fieri, Tyler Florence, or Thomas Keller. Or you can get Famous Dave's Variety Gift Box at Target for a third of the price). Protection also presumes the merit of secrecy.

The ambiguities of legalese notwithstanding, the move for legal protection of recipes is erratic because it uniformly contradicts the notion of secrecy and of sharing. It is no little irony that the recipe for Coca-Cola, one of the most successful commodities ever launched, is not under any form of legal protection but remains a so-called trade secret. On the subject of the Interlude controversy, culinary historian Andrew Smith duly commented that "if an author doesn't want a recipe stolen (or borrowed), then the author should do what Coca-Cola and other commercial companies do with their formula—keep them secret" (Smith 2007). Fair enough, but here we are reminded of one very real dialectic in our media-shared world, which is that modern processes of production are very often equivalent to their communication.

Cantu or any of his colleagues may take steps to safeguard their creations, but they at the same time depend on media exposure—both the literal and the figurative consumption of these creations—to build and maintain their profiles.

Profiles are as important to celebrity chefs as they are to amateur food bloggers. While organizations such as Creative Commons and Electric Frontier Foundation (EFF) embrace the digitization of information as a means of access and of free exchange, including specifically advocating against the authority of obstructive copyright laws, the question of legally protecting recipes challenges this freedom by putting the stress back on personal ownership.[4] The result is not that recipes become unavailable. Quite the opposite: in twenty-first century media culture, everything visible is conceptually available. Food blogs and websites provide ample evidence of this. Rather, what these debates do is to draw attention to personalities who make a display of keeping secrets. Although this territoriality may fly in the face of widespread accessibility, the adage that all publicity is good publicity nevertheless stands. From this perspective, the stamp of the law is less important than the stamp of individuality: here the gastronomic cognoscenti emerge not only as knowing, but as *known*.

Eating a Cantu-branded piece of paper that tastes like cotton candy may not be routine for a majority, but neither is it science fiction. The issue of copyrighting recipes is just one aspect of the kind of branding that defines modern celebrity chefs, whose fame both relies on and is potentially threatened by the competitiveness that animates the food (media) world. As we will see shortly, it is also a notion that is not exclusive to the cognoscenti set. But for now, one useful way to think about some of the differences that we confront in the twenty-first century is that some of the most famously "authored" recipes in history—Câreme's Apple Charlotte, Escoffier's Pêche Melba, and Moisson's Tournedos Rossini, to mention a few, were created to honor not their authors, but other people. This is not to pass judgment on today's chefs for being more self-absorbed, or less humble, than their forebears. To be sure, operating in the cutthroat marketplace of celebrity chefdom (and even "normal" cheffing), they could be forgiven for pursuing personal distinction at almost any cost. But it is perhaps telling of a paradigm shift from a time where self-promotion relied more heavily on potential recognition from wealthy patrons, and homage was a social norm. Today, by contrast, distinction is largely peer based: beyond creating food that paying customers want to eat, a chef's honor comes through recognition by colleagues, sometimes gained through higher accolades such as a James Beard Foundation award or a Michelin star (or several).

An MIT study on intellectual property rights when it comes to sharing recipes and techniques among "accomplished" French chefs (which is to say they had been recognized by Michelin with either stars or forks) found that the chef community largely depended on a "norm-based" honor code rather than any legal intervention. Social norms are those developed and "enforced by a group among its members and generally are developed only for behaviors that are viewed as important by most group members" (Fauchart and von Hippel 2008, 189). The authors found three such governing norms among the chef community: first, that it "is not honorable for chefs to *exactly* copy recipes developed by other chefs"; that "a chef who asks for and is given proprietary information by a colleague will not pass that information on to others without permission"; and finally there is a "right to be acknowledged as the author of a recipe one has created" (193, emphasis in the original). Any violation of these norms would be

> punished by negative gossip within the community, by a related lowering of a violator's reputation, and by a decreased likelihood that additional requests for information will be answered by community members. Famous chefs do not necessarily need to take personal action to ensure that transgressions are noticed and appropriately punished by their community. As one interviewee said, "The community knows my style and can recognize when someone is copying me. Therefore, I do not need to intervene in any way." (193–94)

As Fauchart and von Hippel point out, a similar code appears to hold for the chefs involved in the Interlude controversy: Grant Achatz and Wylie Dufresne did not "need" to intervene, because their community did so on their behalf, and the Australian chef who contravened the anticopying norm was eventually shamed into sending them each a letter of apology. These examples count as good evidence of the suggestion that while digital advances propel us into the "global village," they also rapidly take us back to "life in the small village of several centuries ago" where it is virtually impossible to "engage in social infractions without risking being caught in the act" (Solove 2004, 32).

COOKS SOURCE: MISUNDERSTANDING THE "PUBLIC DOMAIN"

It is undoubtedly a positive development of the food mediasphere that this form of community rallying is not confined to incidences involving "accomplished" chefs, but it is unfortunately also likely that violations of intellectual property outside the professional community are more frequent precisely because the amateur community is as large and varied as it is, and its "norms" are therefore (as yet) tenuous. One case that is sure to have contributed to the establishment of at least one norm regarding copyright infringement involved the now notorious—and also defunct—*Cooks Source* magazine. In its October 2010 "Pumpkin Fest" issue, *Cooks Source* featured an article on apple pie by Monica Gaudio. This attribution was as it should be, except that Gaudio had not given permission for the article to be reprinted (it had previously been published under a different title on a website dedicated to medieval cookery).

When Gaudio contacted the magazine's managing editor, Judith Griggs, requesting an apology (both in print and on its Facebook page, where the piece was also published) and a donation of $130 to the Columbia School of Journalism (which would compensate ten cents per word for the 1,300-word article), Griggs responded by e-mail that it was indeed her "bad" to have overlooked getting permission for the article. "But honestly, Monica," she continued,

> the web is considered "public domain" and you should be happy we just didn't "lift" your whole article and put someone else's name on it! It happens a lot, clearly more than you are aware of, especially on college campuses, and the workplace. If you took offence and are unhappy, I am sorry, but you as a professional should know that the article we used written by you was in very bad need of editing, and is much better now than was originally. Now it will work well for your portfolio. For that reason, I have a bit of a difficult time with your requests for monetary gain, albeit for such a fine (and very wealthy!) institution. We put some time into rewrites, you should compensate me! I never charge young writers for advice or rewriting poorly written pieces, and have many who write for me . . . ALWAYS for free! (quoted in Gaudio 2010)

Griggs did probably not anticipate that Gaudio would publish this communication on her blog, although she perhaps should have. As one Internet professional put it, "If you want something to be private, you must spell it out that it's off the record. And if you're in a dispute with someone, you would not expect an e-mail like (Griggs's) not to become public" (quoted in Kahn 2010).

Not only did the e-mail and the incident become public knowledge, it very quickly went viral and became an Internet meme, with #crooksource and #buthonestlymonica trending on Twitter, where at least five fake accounts took advantage of the scandal to ridicule Griggs and *Cooks Source*, and @RuthBourdain also had his/her say: "Cooks Source never should have stolen those recipes. But let's remember that they are also a victim of theft. Someone stole their apostrophe" (November 6, 2010). On Facebook, angry (former) fans descended on the *Cooks Source* page, a musical rendition of "But Honestly, Monica" soon appeared on YouTube, and as the story hit major broadsheets (including *The Guardian* in the UK), Judith Griggs was rocketed into disrepute. It did not stop there. The day after Gaudio's post, writer and critic Ed Champion (also of *The Bat Segundo Show* fame) revealed on his blog that *Cooks Source* had taken more than just a story about apple pie: Champion posted side-by-side pictures of a recipe for tandoori chicken from the popular blog Simply Recipes, and its exact replication—with the exception of a flipped image—in the *Cooks Source* July 2010 issue (he also noted that its sidebar on garam masala was directly lifted from Wikipedia). At least eight other recipes in that issue had been lifted from unaccredited sources (Champion 2010).[5] Within days, a Google spreadsheet detailing 167 cases of recipes lifted by *Cooks Source* from sources including Martha Stewart, Ina Garten, and *The Joy of Cooking* entered the public domain. By the end of that November, the magazine had folded.

The scandal made it to number four of Robert X. Cringely's "10 dumbest tech moves of 2010" and took the prize as Craig Silverman's "Error of the Year." The blog Smart Bitches Trashy Books coined the verb "griggs," meaning "1. To use content on the web without permission, then request payment from original author for rewrites and editing" and "2. To remain ignorant of plagiarism, ethics, copyright, and asshat behavior" (Wendell [aka "Smart Bitch Sarah"] 2010a). Readers of this blog post were also requested to assist in "Googlebombing" Griggs, which if successful would mean that anyone who entered the search term "Judith Griggs" would be directed to the Smart Bitches page as one of the first links on the Google results page. Within twenty-four hours, the Googlebomb was complete. In a later post titled "Lessons Learned from Cook's [sic] Source," the first lesson listed (albeit in a "not-in-any-particular-order list") was "Do not piss off the inter-net" (Wendell 2010b).

It would be sobering to think that "don't steal"—the second lesson listed by Wendell—would trump pissing off the Internet. Journalist and former Web programmer Ivor Tossel is skeptical:

> It's possible this episode signals that publishers big and small are being put on notice that content theft is unacceptable and will henceforth be vigilantly po-liced by the eye of the crowds. The plague of small northeastern food maga-zines copying articles from websites might finally come to an end.
>
> It's more likely that this serves as a reminder that crowds are attracted to drama above else: drama over principle, drama over consistency, drama over proportion. To revolt against small outrages wherever it's expedient, to laugh at the failings of silly villains when they're available. (Tossel 2010)

At this (relatively) early stage in the social media game, it is impossible to say with certainty which of these two readings is closer to the truth. It is also possible, moreover, that presenting it as an either/or case is a false choice: there is a good chance that "the Internet" got as angry as it did precisely because it was a clear case of "stealing," as in Griggs helping herself without permission to something that belonged to Gaudio. That said, it is equally plausible that Griggs's "haters" were further fueled by her regrettable approach. Tossel put it well when he summarized that "what Judith Griggs is truly guilty of is copyright infringement with a terrible attitude."

The episode does highlight two connected developments that are rapidly gaining center stage in the world of food and social media. The first is about ethics, and the second is about when those ethics apply. While it should ideally not need saying that ethical standards should apply at all times—this is the social norm of "decent behavior," which we would like to think exists across and beyond niche communities—the challenge with the Internet is that not all output is regarded as "serious." Although it is easy to concede that not all output deserves to be regarded as such, or even intends to be, there exists a general perception that people who are not paid for their work—as most food bloggers are not—are simply doing it for fun, out of love, or to take their mind off their boring life (as one reviewer [Slater 2009] characterized Julie Powell's blog project), and therefore that equivalent standards of, say, intellectual property rights do not apply. Judith Griggs was patently of this opinion. But while her transgression is now plain to identify, less obvious are some other situations that raise questions about what can be expected of bloggers and what bloggers can expect of their own endeavors and of each other.

ETHICAL BLOGGING

Developed in 2009, the "Food Blog Code of Ethics" is one manifesto of the ideal social norms of the food blogging community. We will look at the code in closer detail in chapter 4 in the context of amateur restaurant reviewing, but for now Vanilla Garlic blogger Garrett McCord's summary will do: "The general code is don't be an ass, we're a community and you need to respect each other" (quoted in BlogHer Food 2011). As simple (and correct) as this sounds, it does not take account of extra-community interactions, like the situation Amy Sherman (of Cooking with Amy) found herself in when she was contacted by a company that wanted its product featured on her blog. (Both the Food Blog Code of Ethics and the Federal Trade Commission do incidentally require transparency in cases of corporate sponsorship or advertisement, but that was not Sherman's issue.) Said company went on to invite Sherman to an event in Italy where she would be put up in a hotel, with meals, for two days. In return she would be required pay her own traveling expenses and to "cook a unique recipe for 30 to 35 people at the [culinary trade] show." Their thinking was that "you could really generate some nice attention for yourself by blogging about the event. In addition, we would be able to support you through our digital press releases" (quoted in Jacob 2010b).

Sherman declined the invitation but used the opportunity to underline a general industry perception of bloggers as being willing to gain publicity at any cost. ("They would never ask Lidia Bastianich to come to a trade show on her own dime and cook for free. But somehow, it's acceptable to ask bloggers to do this," as she put it.) But she also conceded that the reason this perception exists in the first place is because some bloggers *are* willing to build their profiles at any cost and are happy to provide free publicity. Contrast Sherman's story with that of an Australian blogger who was confused when she was prohibited from taking photographs in a food store. While she could appreciate that "business owners are protective of their business," she could not understand "why they do not see it as a wonderful opportunity to promote their business through online media—for free I might add" (Ladybird 2010). So this is not simply an issue of bloggers alerting industry to the rules of their game, but also of ensuring that those rules are accepted and observed within the community, if indeed a norm-based community is to exist.

Of course, the problem with that consistency is exactly what makes the blogosphere so attractive to so many: there are no *actual* rules. The Web accommodates someone like Ladybird, who presumably blogs as a hobby, as easily as it does the equally fast-growing number of people like Sherman for whom blogging is as professional and serious an undertaking as any other. This overlaps with the similarly contentious question of whether bloggers should be seeking financial compensation for their work. From the perspective of those who do wish make a profession of blogging—which is to say make a living—the answer is an obvious yes. We have already seen examples of successful career bloggers like Ree Drummond, Julie Powell, and Clotilde Dusoulier. Yet in the ocean that is the food blogosphere, they are still just a few waves. Added to this is that for those not lucky enough to secure book deals based on their blogs, when it comes to competing in the marketplace of recipe development, bloggers are still seen as amateurs by at least some industry representatives. According to *Bon Appetit*'s executive editor, Victoria von Biel, for example, who noted that "in blogs, most recipes have been 'adapted from' or 'inspired by,'" most food bloggers do not have the requisite training to develop recipes (quoted in Jacob 2010a). One potential outcome of this is that bloggers end up being able to demand less—if anything at all—for their recipes to be featured in publications besides their own. Yet as food writer Dianne Jacob also notes, "Many food bloggers are honored to be asked for their recipe. . . . No pay is not a dealbreaker." Lack of training notwithstanding, publications like *Bon Appetit* are evidently willing to include more recipes on their website from food bloggers in the future, with the caveat that they will be untested. Ironically, it is precisely the lack of testing by users lacking professional training who then go on to blog about their "adapted" recipes that troubled Zanne Stewart of the erstwhile *Gourmet* magazine in the early days of food blogging: "*Gourmet* has 8 test kitchens and 11 food editors. . . . [it] makes me a bit sad, considering how much work went into the original" (quoted in Barbour 2007).

Circling back to the debate that opened this chapter, adapting and/or taking inspiration from someone else's original work are evidently no less delicate subjects for bloggers than they are for celebrity chefs. A panel discussion dedicated to "Recipe Writing: Copyright, Credit and Etiquette" at the 2011 BlogHer Food Conference in Atlanta highlighted the extent to which best practice norms were as yet unresolved. Dianne Jacob recounted the story of one blogger who had written about a wedding cake that she had found in a published cookbook. She kept the cake's original name but changed some of the ingredients and wrote her own instructions. Because the recipe was presented as "inspired by," and therefore credited to, the original, it was not a case of copyright infringement (she could have requested permission from the cookbook author but was under no legal obligation to do so). What concerned the author was that it was the blogger who received praise for the cake, prompting Jacob to question whether bloggers deserve recognition for recipes they have not written (BlogHer Food 2011). Inasmuch as that question also seems to have an obvious answer—no, they should not—the problem here is in that gray area between writing, developing, and adapting. Does the act of changing ingredients and putting instructions into your own words constitute adaptation? From a legal point of view, we know that lists of ingredients cannot be copyrighted, but that literary expression accompanying those lists can. So once again, if both of those are changed, there is no legal question—and it could even be argued that the new set of instructions represents a work "original" to the blogger. But legalities aside, food writer and publisher David Leite (of the award-winning Leite's Culinaria) sees this example as an ethical issue: "Rewriting is not adapting. Rewriting is only rewriting. . . . Are bloggers that lazy that they can't think of anything original to do? That's not food blogging, that's just re-purposing someone else's work" (BlogHer Food 2011).

Leite may find that not all who engage in it agree with him about what food blogging is or what it should be: just as undergraduate college students are not expected to produce original scholarship, neither can there be a requisite for originality in food and eating from a community made up to a large degree of nonprofessionals who simply like to record and share their culinary adventures—and sometimes banalities. But he did (perhaps grudgingly) acknowledge their importance as the panel concluded:

You [food bloggers] are some of the most powerful people in media right now. The first time a blogger posted a recipe from my site I flew into a fury. I wanted to bring out the lawyers [but] I was told very quietly by my publisher—don't annoy the bloggers they are too important. But don't abuse your power. You can use it for good or you can use [it] for evil. You can be seen as great, or you can be seen as skanks.

We would probably all like to think that the Web is populated by great people, rather than skanks, and to hope that Andrew Keen is wrong about his characterization of Web 2.0 technology as "confusing the very concept of ownership, creating a generation of plagiarists and copyright thieves with little respect for intellectual property" (Keen 2007, 143).[6] The evidence so far does not point to a community of people with obviously evil intent (if that is what "skanks" means). It does, however, paint a picture of a community brought together by a shared love of food but divided on the rules of how best to share it.

Just as some store owners are evidently uncomfortable with the idea of customers taking pictures of their produce, so are some chefs adamant that the food in their restaurants is for eating, not photographing (ergo, not tweeting or blogging about). A roundup of the question of banning photography in restaurants by Zach Brooks (2008) on the Serious Eats blog quotes David Chang, chef-proprietor of Momofuku Ko, where cameras were banned in 2008: "It's just food. Eat it." Brooks reports that other chefs like Mario Batali and Daniel Boulud are more accommodating, stepping in only if the camera (or phone) clicking interferes with other diners' experiences. But for many bloggers, at least half the experience of the meal is in its photographic documentation—or "foodtography" (Wasserman 2011)[7] —even if that means letting the food get cold, or leaving your dining companion alone for an hour while you go home to get the right lens, which a diner at Alinea reportedly did (Murphy 2010). As one writer for Serious Eats put it,

I can totally understand why people wouldn't want food bloggers whipping out their huge-ass cameras during a meal, but in my selfish view, I just really want to take photos in case I want to write about something on my site. The obsessive food blogger part of me (internally) screams, "DON'T EAT UNTIL YOU'VE TAKEN A GOOD PHOTO OF IT!" during most meals. Which is not normal. Thankfully, all my friends know not to eat something until I've taken a photo of it. Sweet Jesus, what's wrong with me? (quoted in Brooks 2008)

A good number of people would likely answer "nothing" in response to this last question, which is to say that, in today's world, this view *is* fast becoming normal. Tucker Shaw, food editor for the *Denver Post* and author of the photographic *Everything I Ate: A Year in the Life of My Mouth* (2005), put it summarily: "It used to turn heads if you took pictures of your food. . . . Now it's ubiquitous and just shows that we are in a spastic food era—we couldn't get more obsessive" (quoted in Murphy 2010). Ethical debates flare up and die down, but clearly standards of "normal" are rapidly changing, and some of those include how to behave at dinner tables. On the subject not of food photography per se, but of whether it is (im)polite to use one's phone at the table, one writer maintains that it is no longer "considered weird at all to pull out your phone. In fact, the situation has sort of reversed itself: you feel awkward if everyone else is using the phone and you're not. . . . Forgive me," he concludes, "but it's Dinner 2.0" (Siegler 2011).[8]

The fact is that a lot of people are doing things very differently from how they would have a decade ago. The Internet and other social media tools like smartphones have made many things much easier, like accessing other people's mouth-watering feasts at the click of a mouse button. In some cases entirely new possibilities have been opened up, like being able to blog about food for a living (one measure of the "mainstreaming" of which is arguably in the 2012 publication of *Food Blogging for Dummies*). Regrettably, these same tools have also made it easier to violate what have been obvious social norms, like taking someone else's output and making it your own without actually doing the work, or (for some) using your phone at the dinner table. But blanket condemnations are always made more difficult by the behavior of crowds: if so many people are doing it, then by being the new normal, perhaps it is acceptable after all? Dishes like molten chocolate cake (invented by Jean-Georges Vongerichten) and fig-and-prosciutto pizza (credited to Todd English) are now "industry staples" (Satran 2011), listed on countless menus without accreditation. Thousands of copyrighted recipes are circulating on the Web, and probably even more that have been legitimized by the phrases "adapted from" or "inspired by." Some of them may be discovered, and villains will be sent to the Internet dogs. But where do we draw the line between questioning the blogger who receives praise for a recipe she did not develop and praising the blogger who cooks her way through one famous book, also known as "cook-through" blogs (The Julie/Julia Project, Alineaphile, Alinea at Home, French Laundry at Home, Tuesdays with Dorie)? Or what of the site, CopyKat Recipes, dedicated to re-creating restaurant dishes at home? There is nothing dubious about any of these projects, excepting perhaps the hero worship in some of the cook-through blogs. But when so much output depends on so much previous output, it is maybe worth remembering a now oft-quoted turning point for Ferran Adrià, that other sometime subject of hero worship. In 1987, Adrià attended a lecture by Jacques Maximin, one of France's most celebrated chefs. Adrià tells the story of someone asking Maximin what defines creativity. "And he just said, 'Not to copy'" (quoted in Gold 2006).

NOTES

1.   The question of food as art is a centuries-old debate. See Korsmeyer 1999 on the historical marginalization of food as an aesthetic category, both by early Greek philosophers, and later in seventeenth-century disputes about still-life paintings so lifelike that they stimulate the appetite rather than the intellect.

2.   Pollack addresses the copyrightability of versions: "To hazard a guess, comparing allegedly infringing works to the archetypical cake, an otherwise identical cake with a filling made of a different type of cherries would be an infringing copy while the cake identical except for a filling made with pears would be an infringing derivative work, as would the same cake in a different shape. An otherwise comparable cake with anchovy filling would not infringe because it is too dissimilar in appeal. As with all other copyrightable subject matter, the court will have to decide at what point in variation a copy supposedly embodying the protected work is a different work, a derivative work, or a compilation including aspects of the work. This may be a practical problem, but it is precisely the problem courts handle now in copyright cases" (Pollack 1991, 14–15). Attorney John T. Mitchell did, however, manage to convince the court that his recipe for scrambled eggs was original enough for copyright. Authored in 2007, the recipe was granted a copyright registration number in 2011. Under the recipe, which can be found on his blog, the author notes that "This copyrighted work of authorship was created for the sole purpose of proving to some dim-witted attorneys that they were wrong to insist 'recipes are not copyrightable'" (Mitchell 2011).

3.   Licensing, patenting, copyrighting, and trademarking are all legally distinct processes but are treated equally here because of their common aim of offering a form of legal protection.

4.   Cofounded by John Perry Barlow, lyricist for the Grateful Dead, the EFF confronts "cutting-edge issues defending free speech, privacy, innovation, and consumer rights today. From the beginning, EFF has championed the public interest in every critical battle affecting digital rights" (https://www.eff.org/about, accessed August 10, 2011).

5.   Ironically, Champion later discovered that parts of an interview he had conducted with Ian Rankin on *The Bat Segundo Show* had been plagiarized by writer (and 2003 "Scottish Journalist of the Year") Jason Allardyce in *The Sunday Times* (Champion 2011).

6.   Keen goes on to cite a 2005 survey that depressingly found that 70 percent of US undergraduates admitted to "some form of cheating," while "77 percent of college students didn't think that Internet plagiarism was a 'serious' issue" (Keen 2007, 143).

7.   Todd Wasserman (2011) reports on Mashable that "at least once a month, 52% of people take pictures with their mobile phones; another 19% upload those photos to the web." Some of these end up on sites like Flickr, where the "number of pictures tagged 'food' increased tenfold to more than six million" between 2008 and 2010 (Murphy 2010). As Michael Antonoff (2011) summarizes the situation in the *New York Times*, "Anyone who eats out is now a potential food critic who can't talk about food without showing it. . . . Is there an appetizer anywhere that isn't available for viewing before eating? Is there a restaurant anywhere where you can dine in peace, without becoming one of the outtakes in someone's photo album?"

8.   See also du Lac 2011 for an account of how more and more people dining alone use digital devices like phones or tablet computers for virtual companionship. While some establishments have no problem with it, others like restaurateur Ashok Bajaj sees the rise of "people texting and doing all this other stuff while they're eating" as a sign that we are "losing" the appreciation of dining out as a special event to be enjoyed on its own merits (quoted in du Lac 2011).

Chapter Three

Twitter Feeding

Too Much of a Good Thing?

In his *Paradox of Plenty: A Social History of Eating in Modern America* (2003), Harvey Levenstein chronicles almost a century (from 1930 to the 1990s) of the American diet, most notably the rise of a postwar food culture characterized by abundance and convenience (Warren Belasco [2006, 47] likewise describes 1950s America as "symbolized . . . by lavish backyard barbecues, fast food hamburgers, and extra-large milkshakes topped with whipped cream"). The paradox that would arise from this plenty is the now well-rehearsed narrative of the consequences of those indulgences on the human body, specifically the obesity scourge that became officialized as an epidemic in 1999 (Levenstein 2003, 259). This book is not (directly) about eating food in the "real" world, but there is an obvious parallel between the convenience culture of food in that world and the abundance of information about food in its virtual counterpart. As we have seen, threats to intellectual property rights are among the challenges that arise from what some would consider too much access in a so-called Information Age. Perhaps it is equally worth considering whether the space where food and social media intersect faces its own paradox of plenty. Is cornucopia always a good thing? And at what point might this trend of people publishing what they cook and eat— including what they are thinking about cooking and eating—miss the point of food as *food*?

35

DIGITAL NARCISSISM AND FOODIE FATIGUE

There is no doubt that a great number of people find some sort of validation and appreciation through sharing stories about food, and that often the communities that grow out of that shared space come to rest on pillars that are stronger than "just" food. Bloggers rallying to Jennifer Perillo's (virtual) side following the untimely death of her husband provide good evidence of this. But looking across the spectrum, there is also a strong likelihood that much of the publication of "self" through food—on food blogs, Twitter feeds and the like—is more in service of what Andrew Keen calls digital narcissism (2007, 55) and what Neal Gabler bleakly dubs the "post-idea world," where knowing something about someone (including publishing information about oneself) trumps "big ideas":

> We prefer knowing to thinking because knowing has more immediate value. It keeps us in the loop, keeps us connected to our friends and our cohort. . . . Few talk ideas. Everyone talks information, usually personal information. Where are you going? What are you doing? Whom are you seeing? These are today's big questions. . . . Instead of theories, hypotheses and grand arguments, we get instant 140-character tweets about eating a sandwich or watching a TV show. . . . We have become information narcissists, so uninterested in anything outside ourselves and our friendship circles or in any tidbit we cannot share with those friends that if a Marx or a Nietzsche were suddenly to appear, blasting his ideas, no one would pay the slightest attention, certainly not the general media, which have learned to service our narcissism. (Gabler 2011b)

It is a somber analysis and hopefully one that is extreme in its defeatism: Marx and Nietzsche were unique in their own time, and there are certainly important thinkers in ours—some of whom are quite adept at expressing their ideas in 140 characters or fewer. But the information we have around us appears so abundant in part because our attention spans are so drastically dwarfed by its volume, which also makes it so much easier to spend the little attention we have on fleeting information ("largely useless," in Gabler's reckoning) rather than on ideas—which may be more useful in the long run.

Consider The Lawrence/Julie & Julia Project. Taking advantage both of the runaway success of The Julie & Julia Project—or more accurately, of the success of the film that resulted from Julie Powell's blog project—and of having "way too much time" on his hands, college student Lawrence Dai committed himself to watching the film *Julie & Julia* every day for one year, and to blogging about each viewing. Unsurprisingly, the novelty soon wore off, and his daily blog posts became dedicated to finding ever more-creative ways to talk about a film that he apparently fast came to despise, thanks largely to his patent dislike of Julie Powell's character. On day 80, he confessed to one recurring worry of this project: that he was spending his days ripping off a film that was based on the life of a real, living person. "But then I got over it," he continues:

> I decided that I wasn't actually personally attacking Julie Powell, but rather "Julie Powell," the fictional version of her that Nora Ephron created for *Julie & Julia*. So that solved a lot of problems. I could feel free to yell at "Julie" all I wanted and I wouldn't have to deal with the fact that I am probably just a **big Internet bully**. Julie Powell is a real person with emotions and feelings, but I wasn't making fun of *her* exactly. No harm, no foul. Right?

Evidently not convinced by his own reckoning, when he discovers (via a reader comment and a subsequent viewing of a YouTube clip of Julie Powell) that the real Julie is not the "bitch" he has decided she is in the film, he has a(nother) fit of conscience: "So now I shudder to think that I might tolerate and even *like* the real Julie Powell. How the fuck do I go back and watch this movie—watch Amy Adams being horrid, . . . watch her drag down each and every scene with her annoying and grating personality—without [sic] the knowledge that the real person may not actually be a monster after all?" "Oh wait, that's right," he finally decides. "She had an **affair** while she was still married to her awesome husband for literary gain. **She *is* a bitch**" (Dai 2011a, emphases in the original).

While one (charitable) reading could take Dai's daily musings as evidence of a leap from gathering information to thinking about it, this is likely only because of the self-imposed *Groundhog Day* quality of his project. With nothing new to take away from the film, he is forced to "think" about what he is doing—though even that endeavor has questionable results, as his tweet from Day 287 confirmed: "Nora Ephron has no new ideas . . . and frankly, neither do I" (September 12, 2011). But the point here is not to think too hard about a project that *Jezebel* questioned as being the "nadir" of stunt-journalism.[1] Dai himself appears well aware of the basic inanity (and arguably, insanity) of his mission, which taught him that "even the stupidest of ideas could find a home on the Internet," as he wrote in his final post (Dai 2011c). What The Lawrence/Julie & Julia Project ironically highlights is the strength—or weakness, if you like—of the cultural capital of food and social media, because it has very little to do with food and everything to do with making a display of the lengths one individual will go to get some attention.

Most tellingly, it works. In addition to being offered a summer job thanks to his blog, Dai has been featured on a number of media platforms, from NPR to the *Huffington Post* to *The Guardian*, where Victoria Beale (2011) predicted that "no doubt Lawrence's room-mate will soon begin blogging about being party to his friend's increasing distress over 365 days—and so on, through a Russian-doll-like progression of postmodern wordpress-hosted carnage as we inch closer to the blogcopalypse." To be sure, the postmodern angle provides endless fodder for this blog about a film about a blog about a book: Dai has been invited into readers' homes to watch the film, after which he blogs about watching the film in those readers' homes. His final viewing was hosted by Off Center @ The Jones, at The Denver Center for the Performing Arts, where members of the public could buy a ticket for $10 and be part of the phenomenon. He is, of course, also featured in this book about food and social media, despite the fact that The Lawrence/Julie & Julia Project is primarily about Lawrence Dai—who at his own admission is no "foodie." Although this example may be extreme, it also highlights the narcissistic and myopic encouragements that social media provide, and that are, as both Keen and Gabler suggest, not so unique after all.

Peeling off one metalayer of the postmodern paradigm, The Julie & Julia Project has not been without its own controversies, some of which re-sketch the divide between food professionals and amateur "foodies." In a blog post that she later describes as having attracted "*all* sorts of haters" (Willis 2011), chef, cookbook author, and former producer of The Travel Channel's Epicurious shows Virginia Willis wrote about "Julia and Julie: Yes, the Swap is Intentional":

> People who happen to eat and are able to type are now our new food experts. The incredible proliferation and self-indulgent blabber of many food blogs has given people the freedom to hallucinate, "I can type and eat, therefore I am a food journalist"! . . . Think about the food writers who spent their entire careers pursuing real food knowledge and good, sound, cooking fundamentals. Think about writers who wrote real literature *that happened to be about food*: Elizabeth David. MFK Fisher. Anne Willan. The real cooks and writers today, the real experts need to be heard, not just any food blogger armed with an iPhone. (Willis 2009, emphases in the original)

We should note Julia Child's own reaction to Julie Powell's blog, which according to the former's editor, Judith Jones, who read Powell's blog together with Child before her death in 2004, was less than encouraging:

> Flinging around four-letter words when cooking isn't attractive, to me or Julia. She [Child] didn't want to endorse it. What came through on the blog was somebody who was doing it almost for the sake of a stunt. She would never really describe the end results, how delicious it was, and what she learned. Julia didn't like what she called "the flimsies." She didn't suffer fools, if you know what I mean. (quoted in Andriani 2009)

Those with a sense of irony may enjoy the fact that Dai and Child appear to have something in common with regard to their opinions about Julie Powell, as well as the fact that Dai does proclaim on Day 273 that he has "actually learned to cook" (Dai 2011b) through the combined efforts of watching the film and having acquired Child's *Mastering the Art of French Cooking* (notwithstanding that the dish he blogs about making on that day consists of angel hair pasta, hot dogs, and ketchup, which is, as he puts it, "not a real dish"). But these sentiments about the direction of the food blogosphere—specifically about how food blogs somehow diminish the plight of "real" food writers—are by no means limited to Child and Willis, as the lively debates around amateur restaurant reviewing (more about which in chapter 4) in particular illuminate. Unfortunately for those who hold these sentiments, however, they are also quickly marginalized by the sheer number of their targets.

The overwhelming evidence is of the Web as a "democratizing" portal that takes little heed of professionalism, instead providing everyone with a virtual megaphone that they can use to carve out their niche as best possible. The largest measure of success here is not recognition from experts in the field (unless by means of social media, like when a Gordon Ramsay or a Mario Batali acknowledges a request for a tweet), or even a mention in something as "old school" as a book: it is attention from the Web itself. On her blog, What's Cooking In Your World ("Cooking my way through the world's 193 countries one meal at a time: First Stop Afghanistan—Last Stop Zimbabwe"), Sarah Commerford explains that she has "absolutely no professional training as a chef." She admits that the blog, which began as a challenge from her son, "has taken over my life, in a somewhat obsessive, but fun way. . . . I've also connected with a whole group of foodies, friends and awesome supporters from all over the world which is exactly what I hoped for when I posted my first Afghani meal in April 2010."[2] Blogs and social media in this way function as unofficial social experiments: they are not all equally successful, but those that do enjoy a sustained presence do so by generating what one early commentator called "social currency" (Rushkoff 2002), or content that is useful not primarily for its own sake but for generating conversation between people.

Some take the social experiment to greater lengths, as Jonathan Stark did in 2011 with a Starbucks card. With an initial balance of $300, Stark put an image of his Starbucks card online, offering strangers the opportunity to download it to their phones and to buy coffee with it. When the story finally caught the public's attention (thanks to being featured on several national news platforms), more than five hundred people had used the card, but with the surprising twist that they typically added back what they took, resulting in transactions topping $8,000 over the course of a few days. The experiment ended when a now-infamous Sam Odio intervened with his own experiment, which was to track the balance of the card and withdraw funds from it to his own card once it reached a certain limit. Odio's brother reportedly transferred the same amount back to Stark's card, thereby avoiding any charges of outright theft: the Odio experiment was supposedly designed simply to show how unsecure Stark's venture was. Still, as the publication *Good* summarized it,

> The [Stark] experiment delighted thousands of people who saw it as anything from a cool game to a validation of humans intrinsic generosity. . . . The @jonathanscard Twitter stream and Facebook page have become soapboxes for sharing about sharing. Former card users are broadcasting stories about the good deeds they've been motivated to perform and how the project reaffirmed their faith in the kindness of strangers. (Goldmark 2011)

This example speaks to some of the best achievements of social media, which lie in the provisioning of new tools for the kind of collaboration and socializing that most of us enjoy doing anyway. It is moreover quite likely the case that social media tools like Twitter and blogs actually incentivize us to engage in these sorts of activities because we no longer have to go out of our way to be kind or gregarious: the Internet liberates us from the "*tyranny of place*," to borrow a phrase from economist Tyler Cowen. This change, he argues, "represents one of the most significant increases in freedom in human history" (Cowen 2002, 5, emphases in the original). Seen in this light, we are undoubtedly freer than ever. But freedom also needs a particular context— and arguably a certain outcome—to be a positive quality.

For all its well-documented benefits, the freedom of the Web also allows us to indulge in an endless amount of information that is potentially "largely useless," to recall Neal Gabler. Feel free to tune into the @having Twitter feed, for example, and—giving literal weight to the idea of Twitter feeding— witness the ongoing publication from complete strangers about what they are eating at that particular moment. Food Feed, the website behind @having, describes itself as "a service that helps you share your eating habits with everyone, from anywhere" ("*Just be sure Mom doesn't get your feed*," they add).[3] Here you can also enter search terms to find other @having followers who have eaten, say, salad, or burgers. How exactly this constitutes a "service" is difficult to determine, unless providing mundane distractions counts as a service today. But indulging us with distractions is clearly some (large) part of the appeal, and not everyone sees this as a bad thing. When the *Los Angeles Times*' Daily Dish blog launched a #weekendeats Twitter hashtag, they invited followers to join them "bright and early Monday morning for #weekendeats, when we waste company time talking about what we ate this weekend, and swapping pictures" (Lynch 2011a).

That is not to say it is all a waste of time. Twitter is interesting and unusual for being one of the most "constrained" social media tools thanks to its 140-character limit, and there are numerous examples of people finding ever more-creative ways to circumvent that constraint. The trend of "twe-cipes," for example, features entire recipes in a space that would not even accommodate a typical ingredient list of a "traditional" recipe. Pioneered by Maureen Evans in Ireland, the @cookbook feed (now inevitably followed by several others) lists recipes that read like cryptic verse: "Honeyed Tagine: brwn lb/500g yam or lamb/T oil&butter/t tumeric&ging&s+p&cinn; +c onion&carrot9m; +c broth/3T honey/9prune. Cvr~h@400F/205C." In a *New York Times* profile, Lawrence Downes asks the obvious: "You're already on the Internet, so why not get the whole recipe, with pictures, and maybe a video? . . . why risk clarity and comprehension for the sake of Twitter's 140-character straightjacket?" Trying some of them for himself, he concludes that there is no good answer, "other than to say it's fun to decode and cook Ms. Evan's tweets. They're a pleasure to look at—strangely absorbing, like bonsai or Fabergé eggs. And (not to spoil the surprise) they work" (Downes 2009).

Twecipes (now also available in hardcopy in *Tweet Pie: The World's Shortest Recipe Book*), like links to traditional recipes with pictures and videos, and like food blogs, clearly serve a purpose that is both functional and fun, if they get people into their kitchens, or at least talking about food, and communicating their experiences in innovative ways. Nevertheless, here again looms what some would call the threat of just too much talk about food. In food writer and cookbook author Amanda Hesser's view, "Having more people interested in good food is never a bad thing." But she has less time for people who "only want to talk about food and every place where they ate, like, doughnuts or something, and where the best doughnuts are secretly found. . . . That cataloguing of food experience is becoming tiresome." Hesser was quoted in a *Chicago Tribune* article titled "Foodie fatigue" by Christopher Borrelli (2010), who subheads the piece "A plea for calm among foodies from a part-time food writer who's part of the problem." Although Borrelli's article is mainly focused on the perceived snobbery of the "foodie" culture, and therefore belongs to the "foodie backlash" that has gained particular momentum in recent years,[4] "being part of the problem" aptly summarizes the what I call the paradox of plenty of social media: in order to reap its benefits, you have to take part, and by taking part you risk either exposing yourself to too much of this good thing, and/or contributing to the same.

In his rant against the new ubiquity of food trucks, which went from being "construction site staples to foodie obsession overnight," *Bon Appétit*'s Jason Kessler similarly bemoans what happened after the initial success of the Kogi truck (one of the original gourmet food carts):

> It [the Kogi truck] capitalized on the burgeoning social media scene to make eating an event. People (read: hipsters) lined up for hours to devour the kimchi quesadillas that all their friends were blogging about. There was a community element to it. There was a sense that something was *happening*. And then, like

all good things, it turned into just another way for enterprising individuals to make a quick buck. You like Kogi? Great. Now there are five Kogi trucks. You like Korean-Mexican fusion? Awesome. Enjoy the stream of Korean-Mexican imitators that cropped up, not to mention Chinese-Mexican, Indian-Mexican, and Native American-French Canadian (totally made-up, but doesn't fry bread poutine sound amazing?) The movement became commodified and now it sucks. (Kessler 2011, emhasis in the original)

He concludes thus: "Now, excuse me, I have to go find some fry bread poutine before this afternoon's cat circus." So, while the choice to filter information is also part of the freedom of the Web—we are the masters of what and who we follow—it is often the case that we expose ourselves to too much before we are able to acknowledge the excess. Like only realizing we have eaten too much after that last slice of pie on Thanksgiving Day, fatigue cannot really be the responsibility of anyone but ourselves, and neither can we expect other people to stop (eating, tweeting, blogging, visiting food trucks) because we are tired of doing so ourselves.

HEALTH AND SOCIAL MEDIA

The paradox of plenty is not confined to fatigue or to so-called information overload. It can equally be a problem of simply choosing to pay attention to the wrong sort of information or of using information in the wrong sort of way. Some followers may find inspiration from following the tweets of @brianstelter25, which track the daily food intake and weight-loss (including occasional weight-gain) details of Brian Stelter, a journalist for the *New York Times*. Following the maxim of holding oneself accountable through publicity (and appropriately to the social media context, Stelter uses the Withings Wi-Fi body scale, functions of which include sending automated daily measures straight to the computer or iPhone), his Twitter page describes the feed as "a personal account about healthy eating and exercise." Yet in a world where the boundaries between personal and public are blurring at a dizzying speed, it is easy to imagine a follower misinterpreting Stelter's personal account as a method approved for public practice. Fortunately the daily habits of someone like Stelter are not particularly radical in either direction and therefore unlikely to encourage any behavior that could be directly harmful. In fact, several of his days do not appear to be those of a dieter, such as August 16, 2011, on which he consumed—taking up three tweets—"yogurt (80 [calories], F1 bar (90), coffee (100) 1/2 roast beef on flatbread, no cheese (300); carrots (15), grapes, apples (50), coffee, 1 cookie (200); coffee (30); 12" turkey/ham (500), apple slices (35); 3 glasses white wine (300); 1/2 small cheese pizza (500?), 1/2 pint Ben & Jerry's froyo (480)".

But there have been other examples of more troubling behavior on Twitter, like the controversy that erupted in early 2011 when Kenneth Tong, a former Big Brother UK contestant, tweeted (to his more than fifteen thousand followers) a number of statements endorsing what he called "managed anorexia," and punting his "Size Zero Pill." Reactions were swift and plentiful, including from celebrities like Gordon Ramsay, who sent out a tweet confirming that he did "not support kenneth tong's campaign"; and singer Rihanna, who claimed that "girls are dying all over the world because of ignorant individuals like this" (both on January 8, 2011)—all incidentally retweeted by @MrKennethTong himself. The public outrage was so acute, including calls for Tong to be barred from Twitter and that his "free speech be blocked," that *spiked* editor Brendan O'Neill suggested that "the reaction . . . was far more unhinged than anything said or done by Tong himself. . . . Yes, Tong wrote a lot of nonsense," he conceded, "but what was far more nonsensical was the idea that his pronouncements, of 140 characters or less, threatened to condemn teenage girls everywhere to a life of starvation as they desperately tried to conform to the preferred body shape of an idiot blogger most famous for having been on Big Brother" (O'Neill 2011).

The reactions themselves testify to one clear positive with social networks: as much as they may facilitate the rapid spread of nonsense, their readers can equally function as a swift correctional resource.[5] Even O'Neill's response points to the (ideal) limitations of social media. Yet we cannot discount the possible harmful effects that someone like Tong could have on those who might be predisposed to taking bad advice (for instance, those who already suffer from an eating disorder or negative body image), even if he is just an "idiot blogger." Witness some of the "thinspiration" he provided:

> @CarolluvsMJJ I like the advice of @MrKennethTong because I'm fat and want to be skinny. I've tried it the healthy way and it didn't work for me. Sorry.

> @shannafraser @MrKennethTong Iv [sic] Lost 3 Pounds in 4 days thanks to you Kenneth I needed to realis [sic] that thin is fashion and you cant [sic] hide behind curvy thnx

> @OhGeeItsMolliee @MrKennethTong I just read your tweet: "What's in your lips today is in your hips tomorrow." It put me off my chocolate. thanks. (quoted in Brassfield 2011)

To add insult to this apparent injury was Tong's subsequent confession (via Twitlonger, an application that allows users to go beyond the 140 character limit) that the whole thing was a hoax. He explained:

It came about after an interesting discussion I had with a friend of mine. The discussion centered round whether it was possible, to go from nowhere to be a globally recognized figure within a week harnessing the power of the internet and specifically Twitter, which I have always maintained is a better medium than national TV. My friend said it wasn't possible. I said it was. To prove him wrong, I decided as a hoax to promote via Twitter something that was universally appalling, I chose managed anorexia. . . . The campaign has worked; I have been a Trending topic on Twitter for over a week. I am scheduled to appear on TV, the Press and Radio shows, over the course of the next week: Grazia, Telegraph, The Sun, The Sunday Times etc. Now it's time to come clean and stop the bandwagon.[6]

Part of "coming clean" from what he called "this scientific experiment" involved a "sizable donation" to a leading UK eating disorder charity, including the proceeds from auctioning his "custom iPod Nano watch on Ebay."

Tong's sincerity has naturally been questioned, notably by the journalist Johann Hari, who conducted an interview with Tong hours before his Twitter "confession," and who found someone entirely consistent with the "managed anorexia" campaign, concluding that "Tong seems to genuinely believe now that women should starve to give him a hard on" (Hari 2011a). Given Hari's subsequent fall from journalistic grace following his admission of plagiarism and of manufacturing facts,[7] this particular interview regrettably remains an unreliable guessing game of who is fooling whom. More unsettling are some of Tong's previous proclamations on Twitter, as detailed by the lawyer David Allen Green, blogger for the *New Statesman*, and host of the blog Jack of Kent. The short series of tweets that caused Green particular concern began with Tong's declaration (in direct opposition to Brian Stelter's take on publicity, it could be noted) that, "Truthfully, when you are as wealthy as I am, you can say, do and think anything without penalty, as you have no one to be accountable to." Challenged by a Twitter follower to "break the law let's see what happens," Tong respond with a link to an article reporting that he had been cleared of sexual assault charges. He placed a winking emoticon (";-)") after the link. Green concludes of the episode that "there is no basis, other than perhaps his tweet, for believing the sexual assault allegations are correct: but his promotion generally of the dangerous and abusive 'managed anorexia'—and the boastful tweet of that link in particular—would not make me think any less of him than if the allegations were true" (Green 2011).

Lest we get sidetracked into giving Kenneth Tong more attention than he deserves, it is worth stressing that this example is not meant to count as evidence of anything inherently "bad" about the Web or with social media. As Adam Geitgey reminded readers in his account of one of the first widely publicized blog hoaxes (involving a fictional girl suffering from, and eventually succumbing to, leukemia), "Remember: the Web isn't evil, evil people are evil" (2002, 89).[8] But it is sadly also the case that vulnerable people are vulnerable, and that the Web's unique capacity for encouraging homophily (the "birds of a feather" phenomenon described in chapter 1, which includes our tendencies to confirmation bias and to using the availability heuristic)[9] is well documented in the rise of what are known as "pro-ana" (pro-anorexia) virtual communities.

The evidence for any direct causal links between media consumption (reading one of Tong's tweets, say) and the development of eating disorders remains inconclusive (Radford 2007; Levine and Murnen 2009). Yet there is ample confirmation that the Web provides community space for people (mostly adolescent girls) who already try their best not to eat—much like, in another context, it provides community space for people who celebrate food by publishing what they eat. An earlier study in *Pediatrics*, for instance, found that the ratio of pro-ED (eating disorder) sites to pro-recovery sites was five to one, but also noted that "a substantial percentage of pro-recovery site users also reported learning about new weight-loss or purging techniques and diet aids as a result of pro-recovery site visitation and later implementing these techniques. This underscores the dangers of online forums where, regardless of original intent, teens can share useful or harmful information with ease" (Wilson et al. 2006, 1641). Later studies confirm that pro-ED sites "present graphic material to encourage, support, and motivate site users to continue their efforts with anorexia and bulimia" (Borzekowski et al. 2010). These efforts are also referred to as "negative health behavior" (Haas et al. 2011), particularly when it comes to provisioning people with so much information as to create the "expert patient" who uses her (largely Web-based) knowledge to "reject and resist mainstream models of health and illness" (Fox et al. 2005). Not restricted to pro-ED sites, these are also the subjects of a number of YouTube "thinspo" clips and Facebook groups sharing pictures and advice like "Skip dinner, be thinner (literally)."[10]

Although negative Web behaviors, like those involving identity fraud, "sock-puppeteering" (the practice of assuming an anonymous online identity, typically in order to direct "third-party" praise at oneself), vitriolic comments, challenges to intellectual property rights, and so on, have received a fair amount of publicity generally, relatively little attention is paid to the sorts of behaviors that could have negative impacts on people's health and well-being when it comes to food and social media. To not include the not-so-hidden underground of eating disorders when celebrating (or even lamenting) the abundance of "foodie-ism" on the Web could indeed count as evidence of the blinkered perspective of that particular community. But just as hunger and obesity are considered opposite poles of the same spectrum, so too do eating disorders exist on a continuum that shares with foodie-ism an obsession with all things food, albeit for radically different reasons. Still, some evidence does exist that in their community provision, these sites are also important for providing a safe space where sufferers can find advice and support that is free of the stigma they may encounter in more general health forums (Dias 2003; Mulveen and Hepworth 2006).

Moving away from eating disorders specifically, when it comes to blogs related to health issues, the authors of one study maintain that blogging for "better health," as they call it, is both "ego gratifying and behaviourally empowering in a manner that allows users with health problems to tackle their illnesses and pursue creative outcomes proactively. As a vehicle of mass communication, blogs offer lurkers a strong bandwagon heuristic with which to evaluate the flood of health-related information available on the web." They conclude that "blogs epitomize the 'public-ness' in public health" (Sundar et al. 2007, 86). (These findings give humorous relief to a Twitter exchange in March 2011 between celebrity chef Jamie Oliver and one of his fans, @Adam9309, who tweeted to the chef that "I've been blogging for 199 days, and tried to get healthier. I've failed miserably so far—it's time for a billing change!" Oliver responded with the question, "Does blogging make u healthy?") A more recent study undertaken by scientists at Johns Hopkins University focused on Twitter as a public health tool. Using an algorithm to filter keywords from two billion tweets over a period of seventeen months, they were able to tracks things like flu and allergy patterns and also tweets related to obesity.[11] Their findings, summarized in *The Atlantic*, suggested that in the case of obesity, "People are sharing information about their weight and health through Twitter. Social media may contribute to the success of future obesity interventions" (Villarica 2011).

One such intervention is headed by Jamie Oliver, as watchers of his ABC series *Jamie Oliver's Food Revolution* will be aware. The TV show laid the foundation for what has continued as essentially a social media movement using both Twitter (#foodrevolution), where the Food Revolution team also hosts regular Twitter "parties" (#foodrevparty); and Facebook, where people can "like" the "Food Revolution Community" group. Launched in March 2010, Oliver's Food Revolution is "about saving the health of America's next generation. Kids need better food at school and better health prospects. We need to keep cooking skills alive. Stand up and be counted—you have the power to make a difference."[12] People are invited to "stand up" by signing the Food Revolution petition, which allows them to be in the company of celebrities like Robert Downey Jr., Elton John, Jennifer Aniston, and Eva Longoria, to name just a few of many. Aimed at one million signatures, the petition needed approximately 225,000 supporters to reach its target as of January 2012.

Jamie Oliver is arguably one of the first of a now-growing group of celebrity chefs who have taken on roles as social activists, and particularly in the context of obesity and school nutrition. He was the first chef to be awarded the prestigious TED (Technology, Entertainment, Design) prize in

2010, his wish being to "teach every child about food and fight obesity." Oliver's concerns have also been recognized by Ban Ki-moon, the UN secretary-general. During the first live "Ask the Secretary-General" global social media conversation in September 2011 (as part of that year's UN summit focusing on noncommunicable diseases [NCDs]), Ban answered a question sent in by Oliver asking how to reduce the figure of 35 million people who die of NCDs—obesity among them—every year. (Oliver had a few days earlier sent the secretary-general an open letter expressing the same.) Ban agreed on air that it was an "unacceptable" situation and cited a number of lifestyle changes as key to saving lives. Moderator Juju Chang confirmed that "Lifestyle diseases, very true, that's an initiative very dear to Jamie Oliver's heart."[13] On Jamie Oliver's website, the Food Revolution Team took the opportunity to urge readers to support the UN summit, providing both letter templates to be used to request heads of state to attend the summit, and a sample tweet: "UN Sec Gen: Will you hold world leaders accountable for outcomes of #UNSummit on #NCDs? #FoodRevolution [PLEASE RT]" (insertion in the original).[14]

Like the question of whether Google is making us stupid (Carr 2010b), the issue of the actual potential for social media to incite change is topical, particularly in the wake of the so-called Arab Spring when social networking seemed to play an instrumental part in a number of uprisings in the Arab world. It is also a very debatable topic, featuring regular disagreements between writers like Clay Shirky (2008, who argues that "unorganized" social media networks have surpassed in influence the role of formal, organized institutions) and Malcolm Gladwell, whose view is summarized in the subtitle of a *New Yorker* piece: "Why the revolution will not be tweeted" (2010). The point here is not to join these debates or to assess the likelihood of Jamie Oliver's success. It is instead to use these health-related examples to illustrate two notable phenomena: first, that in addition to their providing "social currency"—in other words, getting us to have conversations—social media have fast become tools for much more serious pursuits (successful or not), like health interventions and organizing antiobesity campaigns. The second relates more directly to the concerns of this chapter, which is the more contentious issue of whether more attention is always a good thing.

PARADOX OF PLENTY

There can be little argument against raising awareness about preventable and potentially life-threatening conditions like obesity. But as with debates around professional versus amateur restaurant reviewing, or food writing, or even the rights of an "idiot blogger" like Kenneth Tong to promote what he likes on Twitter, one consequence of the ubiquity of data on the Web is, as Neal Gabler (2011b) put it, "Everyone talks information," but (relatively) few question the veracity of that information, or the authority of who is delivering it.[15] Jamie Oliver's qualification as a chef makes him an authority on preparing food, but it does not qualify him as an authority on NCDs or on how to prevent them. Even as some elements of his movement have obvious merit (such as campaigning for more nutritious foods in schools), his approach is one that risks simplifying a complex public health situation and thereby simplifying how his followers think about the same issue. When he delivered his TED talk in February 2010, Oliver began with the depressing statistic that "in the next eighteen minutes when I do our chat, four Americans that are alive will be dead from the food that they eat."[16] Not only are these figures questionable (Rousseau 2012), but this statement also misrepresents the solution to the obesity "epidemic" (for which there exists no scientific consensus, it should be noted) as a simple case of food regulation: ban flavored milk in schools! Stop eating junk food! Yet as a cardiologist questions in *The Atlantic* (acknowledging first the multiple nonfood-related factors that can contribute to unintended weight gain):

> Should we regulate choices through a method like the institution of a fat tax? On what then? A fast-food burger? Then what are you taxing? The entire product. Should all burgers be banned? A particular component? If so, which one? The bread? The vegetable condiments? The meat? Do we tax all meat? Is it some particular meat combination? Who decides, and based on what? . . . Addressing complex relationships requires a thoughtful and coordinated plan. Rapid implementation of oversimplified approaches for the sake of expediency of political purpose is dangerous. It can lead to overarching rules, recommendations, and regulations that can have severe unintended consequences. Albert Einstein noted that we need to make things as simple as possible—but no simpler. We and our relationship to food are simply not simple. (Fenster 2011)

(In his defense, Jamie Oliver would probably not endorse banning all burgers—he did, after all, convince the owner of Patra's Charbroiled Burgers in Los Angeles to introduce a "Revolution Burger" to his menu.)

As this "simply not simple" relationship we have to food implies, acknowledging the complexity of a situation—like how to curb rising rates of obesity—also requires recognizing some ungainly paradoxes in the foodscape that really come to the fore across the spectrum of social media. While Jamie Oliver tries to tweet his way to a food revolution where more people care about "good" food, others lament the foodie (and the food truck) revolution where too many people care to tweet and blog about the same. If some got their way, girls would stop eating altogether, "fat" politicians like Chris Christie would be precluded from consideration for the US presidency (Kinsley 2011; Robinson 2011), while others might settle for certain regulations to pass us into an (unspeakable) future of no fast-food burgers. What then? Would a Kobe beef burger at a Wolfgang Puck restaurant still be acceptable? Or if a national tax on soda were to be implemented, what about a homemade root beer bundt cake with root beer fudge frosting?

If for some reason you cannot eat any of these items yourself, you can look at images of both the burger and the cake on Tastespotting, an "obsessive, compulsive, collection of eye-catching images that link to something deliciously interesting on the other side."[17] The "other side" here refers to the particular blog that originally featured the image and that was in turn lucky enough to be featured on Tastespotting, considered the "gold standard of websites that show images of food" (Lynch 2011c). There are naturally others, like Foodgawker, Foodspotting (which also offers Cartspotting), Dessertstalking, and Yeastspotting, not forgetting Tastestopping, which provides a home for pictures of food rejected by other sites. If you like pictures of outlandish greasy and/or large portions, you can visit This Is Why You're Fat (or buy the book). For close-up cross-sections of sandwiches, visit Scanwiches (or buy the book). If you prefer cross-sections of candy bars, check out Scandybars (not yet available as a book).

If we judge our freedom by what the Web and social media make available to us, it is a chaotic and contradictory liberty. We are free to eat and to tweet about it, but we should also try to curb our enthusiasm for hearing the sounds of our own virtual voices. If we belong to a group identified as "at risk" of being a public health burden, or a poor role model, we should be less free to eat, but we are welcome to gawk at pictures of everything we should not be enjoying on a website that reminds us why we are fat. And yet, although the tensions between eating and not eating that permeate the virtual world of food may seem to give the lie to any inclusive nationwide community, there remains a strong narrative thread through it all, which is a seemingly boundless obsession with food. Different kinds of food, yes—even different classes of food. But virtual food in all its shapes, sizes, and variations on fat content reflects an astonishing appetite for thinking about food. Perhaps Hannah Hart of the blog My Drunk Kitchen said it best on behalf of the nation—excepting maybe vegans—in her rap number "Show Me Where Ya Noms At" ("noms" being slang for food, the rap satirizes the fact that everyone now seems to cultivate a culinary obsession) in which she tells us that all her fantasies involve cheese.[18] Then again, who is to say that vegans do not fantasize about (real) cheese? Some of us enjoy thinking most about what we cannot, or should not, have. The Web has it all, and then some. You should also feel free to decide that plenty might be too much.

NOTES

1. http://jezebel.com/Lawrence-Julie-Julia-Project (accessed January 15, 2011).
2. http://www.whatscookinginyourworld.com/ (accessed August 30, 2011).
3. http://www.foodfeed.us/ (accessed August 30, 2011).
4. See, for example, Katharine Shilcutt's "Has the 'Foodie' Backlash Begun?" (2010); B.R. Myers's "Moral Crusade Against Foodies" (2011); and Robert Sietsema's response to the latter, "Yes, Foodies Are Ridiculous. But Then So is B. R. Myers!" (2011). On the tension between democracy and distinction in modern foodies, see Johnston and Baumann 2010. On "foodie fatigue," see Nichols 2011.
5. In the case of potentially damaging Internet rumors, author and professor of law Cass Sunstein (2010, 102) proposes that the otherwise contentious "chilling effect" (historically used to describe instances of censorship and the gagging of free speech) could be optimized to produce the situation in which "some falsehoods are useful for producing the truth." For one reaction to what is characterized as this "despicable" idea, see Lasky 2009.
6. http://www.twitlonger.com/show/82t0bf (accessed January 17, 2011).
7. For his public apology detailing his transgressions (including substituting interviewees' spoken words with extracts from their published works, and editing Wikipedia articles for purely self-serving and/or malicious reasons), which ironically mirrors Tong's own confession, see Hari 2011b.
8. Hari (2011a) reaches a similar conclusion to the Tong saga: "So what can we learn from the twisted Twitter-parable of Kenneth Tong? It seems that of [sic] you drill down into women's insecurity and men's misogynies, even a talentless, spoiled little sociopath can catch the attention of the world, for a few days. It may be new media, but it's an old, old story."
9. Coined by psychologists Amos Tversky and Daniel Kahneman (1974), the availability heuristic refers to the rule of thumb many of us use to make decisions based on how much information about a particular phenomenon we have available to us. Following the attacks of 9/11, for example, many people chose to drive rather than to fly because the mediascape was replete with scare stories about flying, even though driving is statistically more dangerous than flying. Similarly, if you choose to only pay attention to viewpoints that mirror and reinforce your own, you unsurprisingly have available a fount of evidence to corroborate any decisions based on those viewpoints.
10. See also the UK documentary *The Truth About Online Anorexia* (2009), available on YouTube: http://www.youtube.com/watch?v=PnR-PxboxdI (accessed August 13, 2011).
11. The authors of the paper do acknowledge limitations with filtering tweets using keywords only, using the examples of, "I'm *sick* of this," and more humorously, "justinbeber [sic] ur so cool and i have beber*fever*" (Paul and Dredze 2011).
12. http://www.jamieoliver.com/us/foundation/jamies-food-revolution/our-campaigns (accessed September 10, 2011).
13. http://www.unmultimedia.org/tv/webcast/2011/09/live-global-conversation-with-the-un-secretary-general-on-social-media.html (accessed September 30, 2011).
14. http://www.jamieoliver.com/us/foundation/jamies-food-revolution/news-content/the-1st-un-summit-on-non-communicable-di (accessed September 12, 2011).
15. One Australian survey found that more than half the population turn to "Dr. Google" for self-diagnosis of medical problems, many results of which are misleading, if not outright dangerous, as in the case of unsupported claims of the link between child vaccination and autism (Dunlop 2011).
16. http://www.ted.com/talks/jamie_oliver.html (accessed September 30, 2011).
17. http://www.tastespotting.com/about (accessed September 10, 2011).
18. http://hartoandco.com/show-me-where-ya-noms-at.html (accessed November 10, 2010). For a take on why Americans sing about food, see Rogers 2012.

Chapter Four

Everyone Is a Critic (but Who Is This "Everyone"?)

In 2007, when Gordon Ramsay was getting ready to open his first New York restaurant, Gordon Ramsay at the London, he acknowledged the fact that his success largely depended on the opinion of one man: Frank Bruni, then the restaurant critic for the *New York Times*. Joking that he was considering getting pillowcases made for his staff with a picture of Bruni's face so that they would recognise him, Ramsey also conceded that "the *New York Times* is a different sort of thing to what goes on in Britain. There's real integrity to it. He [Bruni] even goes to the lengths of being made over, so people won't spot him" (quoted in Rayner 2006). A few months later, and after having been given a mere two stars (out of four) by Bruni, Ramsay changed his tone dramatically:

> The fat, lazy thing about Frank Bruni was all the seedy, undercover blog bullshit. I don't give two fucks about it. Never have; never met the guy; not even remotely interested. I'm being judged on my persona as opposed to my food, and you know what? Fuck it. The thing I find fascinating is, what qualifications do you need to become a food critic then? None. Good luck to them. (quoted in Thompson 2007)[1]

Bruni's credentials would be questioned again shortly thereafter when he gave Jeff Chodorow's Kobe Club zero stars thanks to food that was "disappointing, even infuriating" (Bruni 2007b). Chodorow responded with a full-page "letter to the editor" in the same periodical, in which he insinuated that the review was a series of "personal attacks" and challenged the culinary expertise of what he called "your 'critic'" (Bruni had previously worked as a political correspondent in Rome): "Your readers would not expect your drama critic to have no background in drama or your architecture critic to not be an architect. For a publication that prides itself on integrity, I feel your readers should be better informed as to this VERY IMPORTANT fact, so that they can give your reviews the weight, or lack thereof, they deserve" (Chodorow 2007).

Chodorow and Ramsay are naturally not the first restaurateurs to smart from negative reviews (and Chodorow would take out another advertisement in the *Times* after yet another poor review by Bruni, this time of his Wild Salmon restaurant).[2] Neither are they the first to underestimate the voice of the media. As former *Times* critic Mimi Sheraton responded to the Chodorow debacle:

> Chodorow, of course, was an idiot to have run such an ad. For one thing, it does worlds of good for the critic, indicating he or she has a strong following, and that his or her words can make or break a dining place—in itself a measure of proven dependability. . . . But the most damaging result to Chodorow's restaurant from his blow-up is the added exposure of the negative review to so many who may never have read the original. . . . Frank Bruni will have the last word, of course, as we in the press always do. (Sheraton 2007)

Sheraton might be correct in her concluding remark, but with the caveat that it is no longer clear which "press" will have that last word. Indeed her use of the term "the press," with its already-archaic ring, is telling of some of the major shifts that have happened, particularly in the world of restaurant reviewing. The authority of the print press has given way to online media, and the last-word authority of those (like Bruni) employed by media outfits are relentlessly challenged by the voices of anyone with a blog or a Yelp or Urbanspoon account who also wants to review restaurants, and who is often more content with having the first word than the last.

REVIEWING ETHICS

The main narrative around social media and food criticism concerns the fact that, as the saying now goes, everyone is—or at least can be—a critic. The social mediascape has spawned the "Age of the Appetite," as Irish food critic Trevor White dubs it, and here "the diner has *become* the critic, and the critic had better take stock of the change" (White 2007, 21, emphasis in the original). Which means that people whose (paid) job it is to write restaurant reviews are now competing with an army of bloggers, most of whom do it for free, and some of whom, most contentiously, do it in return for free meals. This has led to a number of debates around the ethics of criticism, including when it is appropriate to review a newly opened restaurant, whether a chef should respond to a negative review, whether reviewers should always dine anonymously, whether accepting "freebies" or "comped" meals is acceptable, and not least about what qualifies anyone to be a critic, now that everyone theoretically can be one. The simplified—and sometimes simplistic—version of this narrative is that amateur critics cannot be trusted because they are, well, amateurs.

Curiously, though, more than a few of the controversies that have come to light as examples of unethical behavior have involved professional critics, meaning here people who are in fact paid to visit restaurants and to write about their experiences. Veteran food columnist for *Esquire* John Mariani (also chief editor of the "Virtual Gourmet" newsletter), for instance, has been accused of blurring ethical and professional lines for accepting comped meals and travel expenses from restaurants, some of which he then included in his annual "Best New Restaurants" list (Martelle 2005).[3] When author and *Time* columnist Josh Ozersky got married in 2010, he was also accused of unprincipled behavior following his article on "Great Wedding Food: Tips from a Newly Married Critic." After describing a menu comprising his "favorite dishes from half a dozen restaurants," including mention of each of the chefs who had cooked the food, his main advice was to "Forget the caterer! Plug directly into the source of your hometown's culinary delights, and happiness, enduring and radiant, will immediately follow" (Ozersky 2010).

Ozersky was taken to task as the addressee of an "open letter" by food critic Robert Sietsema in the *Village Voice* questioning whether the food had been paid for by money or publicity, and highlighting how the account misrepresented the job of a food critic:

> One of the assumptions the reader might make is that you'd promised these chefs, many of whom do high-end catering and expect big bucks for it, to mention them in your magazine column. . . . The most painful part of the article for me is the headline, in which you declare yourself a food critic. Since the function of a critic, anonymous or not, is to eat food and render an unbiased opinion, you seem to have failed on that account with your unstinting praise for your own wedding banquet. And remember, you're addressing literally millions of uninitiated readers, and giving them the false impression that food journalism operates via palsy-walsy contacts among chefs and the journalists who write about them. (Sietsema 2010b)

Ironically for the man who had previously described Adam Roberts (of The Amateur Gourmet blog) as a "world-class mooch" for having accepted a free dinner at Alain Ducasse in New York (Moskin 2010), Ozersky was forced to add a disclaimer to his original article explaining that he had, in fact, not paid for any of the food (or even the venue, provided gratis by Jeff Chodorow), and also that his title was a misnomer because he is "not an anonymous critic" and does not "review restaurants for TIME (or anyone else)."

The subject of the "palsy-walsy" relationship between chefs and people who write about food has come under particular scrutiny in recent years, perhaps as a consequence of the fact that there is so much publicity about food but a relative scarcity of assurances about exactly what kind of publicity (read: unbiased or sponsored) it is. Sietsema is clear in his separation between professional and amateur behaviors, describing as a "nebulous area of quasi-journalism" (quoted in Moskin 2010) the common restaurant practice of comping meals in return for publicity, as well as the increasing boldness of food bloggers and restaurant guides in demanding free meals in return for writing about them. Yet these practices also contribute to a general climate of suspicion where perhaps none is due. When Meridith Ford Goldman, former food critic for the *Atlanta Journal-Constitution*, wrote in that periodical about her own wedding celebration, at least one writer was quick to label as a "conflict of interest" the fact that some of the food was catered by a chef whom Ford Goldman had recently given a glowing review, and that in her article, she "offered kind words (read: *favourable, free publicity*) for three other chefs with whom the wedding couple did business" (Edelstein 2008, emphases in the original). This despite the fact that the original article contained the disclosure that "we paid full price for our wedding and every delicious morsel our guests enjoyed" (Ford Goldman 2008).

Although the Ozersky controversy was arguably a clearer case of an ethical misstep, both that example and the one of Ford Goldman's wedding highlight a fundamental dilemma in the world of food criticism: it is a professional practice dedicated to the pursuit of a pleasure that is both personal and highly contextual.[4] Even so, the critics most dedicated to the professionalism of that practice cannot be 100 per cent objective, or a *homo economicus* (the ideally rational person who economists used to wish we could be)—and why would they be? Nobody wants to read a review written by a robot. We want human accounts written by humans. And being humans, critics have preferences, biases, and fallibilities. This does not excuse corrupt behavior where it can be avoided—and there is no question that it should be avoided at all costs—but it does make it more difficult to answer a question like the one headlining one summary of the Ford Goldman affair: "Is it wrong for a food critic to hire local chefs to cater her wedding?" (Romenesko 2008). In one respect, the answer is easy: certainly not. In her private capacity she has the right to hire whomever she likes to cater her wedding, and being in the business of food criticism, it is entirely reasonable for someone like Ford Goldman (or Ozersky, or countless others) to have personal relationships with people in the business of preparing food. But perhaps it is "wrong" to publish details about that private event in her public capacity as a food critic.

The dilemma emerges somewhere in that imprecise zone between the private and the public, and while it may be (relatively) clear how a professional ought to separate the two, that particular lack of clarity is one of the main animating features of social media. Food bloggers who write about restaurants do so explicitly in their capacities as private individuals who have the right to a public voice, and apart from the ego gratification of getting to practice that right, many of them claim to be providing a public service: bloggers write for their readers. Consider blogger Danyelle Freeman, aka Restaurant Girl (and now author of *Try This: Traveling the Globe Without Leaving the Table*). She describes her reviewing policy on her blog (which was "born [in 2006] out of a void: a critic to identify with, someone I could truly relate to"):

> First and foremost: *If you are open for business and charging your clientele full price, you are open to review.* I stand firmly and fully behind my position. With the advent of blogs and instantaneous gratification & news, there has been much controversy over the fairness of such practices. . . . Therefore, I feel compelled to reiterate my policy of review once again: if you are open for business and charging your clientele full price, you are open to judgement. There will of course be tweaks to work out, service kinks, the factors are endless. My responsibility remains exclusivity [sic] to the reader. (Freeman 2008, emphases in the original)

Reiterating her responsibility on the issue of remaining anonymous when reviewing, she explains that she has "no problem in having an open discussion with chefs. I hope to understand their vision, even peek in their kitchens, all in the pursuit of getting a truer picture of the dynamic in both in the front of the house as well as behind kitchen doors. . . . This will not in any way cloud my judgement as my ultimate and exclusive responsibility is to the reader."

Restaurant Girl and blogs like hers—that is, written by "ordinary" people rather than appointed critics—go some way to deconstructing the perceived snobbery of the restaurant scene. More than a decade ago Arthur Schwartz (long-time food editor of the New York *Daily News*, where Freeman incidentally penned a column for two years thanks to her blog) commented that he "wished the dining public trusted their own judgement more. . . . They think they don't know enough. That's because food media and the food word have made it seem very elitist. I'd love to get the elitism out. After all, everyone eats" (quoted in Dornenburg and Page 1998, 229). But to others, that is now exactly the problem. In an article for the *Columbia Journalism Review* titled "Everyone Eats . . . But That Doesn't Make You A Restaurant Critic," Sietsema (2010a) uses the example of Restaurant Girl to describe the "culinary zeitgeist of our era" as one that takes no heed of the ethics of reviewing that Craig Claiborne codified when he took the job as the *Times* critic in 1957. Claiborne's rules included visiting a restaurant at least three times (naturally precluding the kind of "judgment" Freeman insists a restaurant is potentially subject to the minute it opens its doors), anonymously where possible, and never accepting free meals.

Claiborne's standards have since been included in the "Reviewers' Guidelines" section of the Food Blog Code of Ethics (Burton and Greenstein 2009) with various qualifications, like not publishing anything pseudonymously (while respecting the need for anonymity), and the need to disclose any acknowledgment from a restaurant, whether in the form of comped meals, invitations to culinary events, or even being recognized as a reviewer. (When it comes to disclosing freebies, Sietsema notes that "a scan of blogs that review New York restaurants suggests that this is virtually never done." According to the Federal Trade Commission's 2009 Guides Concerning the Use of Endorsements, this is now a punishable offense, with potential fines for both the blogger and the business in question.)[5] In short, the Code of Ethics recommends that bloggers follow journalistic standards of integrity and transparency. As with the example of vituperative comments and anonymous slurs on the Web, accepting and following standards of best practice should hardly be controversial. The main problem here, however, is that food bloggers are not journalists, and social media allow people to make up their own rules as they please. Freeman could not find a voice she could "truly relate to," so she created that voice, and in so doing intentionally set herself apart from the standards of professional restaurant reviewing. Irksome as it may be to professionals like Sietsema (and clearly to others also, like the art dealer who has made Freeman the subject of Twitter and blog parody), she is free to do so.[6]

British food writer Tim Hayward recognizes this dilemma in his response to the Food Blog Code of Ethics:

> I'm a little uncomfortable with the notion of "professionalizing" anything on the web. What we now regard as professions, the law, medicine, banking etc, all began when groups of interested parties set behavioural codes that excluded others in the name of "maintaining standards." There are obvious reasons why some standards should be maintained, but any attempt at creating an ethical elite on the web, in any field at all—particularly food writing which is not, after all, Woodward and Bernstein but people writing about their tea—seems to run counter to the spirit of self-governance, self-publishing and ultimately self-expression. (Hayward 2009)

Hayward's view is not antithetical to Sietsema's, who also notes that he is "all for everyone having his or her say, but when it comes to cultural criticism there is a strong case to be made for professionalism and expertise" (2010a). The proverbial rub, then, is in the distinction—or lack thereof— between food criticism as a form of cultural commentary, practiced and maintained by a group who are recognized experts in the field, and online restaurant reviewing by a group who are fashioning themselves as the new experts at delivering experiences and information, and delivering it *fast*. (In answer to the question of what makes her a restaurant expert, Freeman explains, "Most importantly, I don't over-intellectualize food. I'm a different kind of food writer. I'm an eater.")[7] But as food writer and industry consultant Joyce Goldstein points out, it may be worth remembering the difference between reviewing and criticism: "Reviewing is 'You went, you ate there, and you had a good time, or not.' . . . Criticism implies having a scale of knowledge and having a range of things that serve as a basis for comparison. It involves a certain level of intelligence, a frame of reference, a big picture, and some depth behind the words" (quoted in Dornenburg and Page 1998, 151).

To be sure, the "big picture" could provide one visible heuristic for distinguishing between professional critics and bloggers, the latter of whom almost invariably count on photographs to tell at least some part of their dining experiences, while broadsheet journalists for the most part still generate pictures with words. Distinctions of professionalism aside, there is no question that bloggers have fast gained importance in the field of restaurant reviewing, thanks to attention from both the public at large and restaurants themselves. In his review of the then-emergent (in 2007) trend of blogging about restaurants, Allen Salkin recounts the story of blogger Ed Levine (now of Serious Eats) posting on his blog that he was planning to eat lunch at Thomas Keller's acclaimed restaurant Per Se an hour later. Levine had also noted that for what he was about to pay, he could afford seventy-seven hotdog lunches at Gray's Papaya. During Levine's last course, "the waiters, with a grand flourish, brought out a hot dog. Someone at the restaurant had seen his blog entry only an hour earlier" (Salkin 2007).

This is just one example of restaurants taking note of what bloggers say about them. It is an implicit—in this case a little more explicit—acknowledgment of what Salkin then called the "new food game . . . that never stops grazing. A proliferation of blogs treating every menu revision, construction permit, clash of egos and suspiciously easy-to-get reservation as high drama is changing the rules of the restaurant world and forcing everyone from owners to chefs to publicists to get used to the added scrutiny." (Salkin adds that as a result of blogs operating "apart from the traditional news media . . . ethical standards are all over the map.") Unsurprisingly, not all interactions between restaurants and social media players are as amicable or playful as Per Se's hot dog stunt, such as the case of one bar patron in Houston being told that she needed to "get your ass up and leave the establishment" after she had tweeted that the bartender was a "twerp" and a #jackoff (Huffington Post 2011b).[8]

More reminiscent of the negative publicity that Gordon Ramsay and Jeff Chodorow inadvertently courted in their responses to negative reviews was a case in 2010 involving Ramsay's erstwhile protégé, Marcus Wareing, now chef-owner of Marcus Wareing at the Berkeley in the United Kingdom. The review was written by a blogging duo who call themselves (and their blog) The Critical Couple. They began their review with the declaration that they are "big fans" of the restaurant, which they had visited on six previous occasions. But this time, "sadly, it missed almost all the targets" (TheCriticalCouple 2010). The review itself was less controversial than its metanarrative, which took off when they revealed on the eGullet forum that Wareing had apparently phoned them subsequent to the review and had "ranted . . . for close to 30 minutes" (MrsCC 2010). The post attracted close to a hundred comments over the next few days, many in sympathy with the couple, but plenty questioning their motives—and in turn the broader ethical implications—of publicizing what was ostensibly a private phone call. The story was picked up by Eater and finally featured in the *Guardian* under the titular question "How right is the customer who blogs?" (Hayward 2010), where Wareing was quoted as saying that he was "saddened" to see details of his private conversation made public.

There is, once again, no easy answer to the question that several commenters posed (and answered), namely how *should* this story have proceeded? Some claimed that being regular customers, who had apparently also had more than one friendly conversation with the chef, the couple should have refrained from writing a negative review in the first place and should rather have addressed that evening's faults privately with the maître d' at the restaurant (which "MrsCC" claims did in fact happen). Others read it as an example of the brave new world of citizen journalism where restaurants' flaws must out, nothing is protected by the sanctimony of privacy, and Marcus Wareing should have known better than to trust in such an outdated notion. Plenty doubted the veracity of the phone call at all, calling it a ploy for blog publicity. In the *Guardian* piece, Tim Hayward offered the reading that a "journalist can pretend to be just a customer and a customer, these days, can express their opinion as if they were a journalist—but it's difficult to claim to be both, simultaneously with any degree of credibility." He also offered "the alternative analysis":

> [T]hat this is a ridiculous storm in a teacup. The Critical Couple will gain publicity for their new site as a result of this, Wareing will lose no business whatsoever. No food blog can seriously affect a restaurant's success and so the only thing more deluded than many bloggers' own illusion of power is the paranoia of chefs, Googling themselves in the lonely hours between service. (Hayward 2010)

This reading is certainly a possibility and very likely the correct one in this particular example. But in general it ascribes too much predictability to a playing field that has already shown itself to be highly unpredictable, thanks at least in part to the challenges to traditional power structures that social media bring.

For one thing, if professional reviews can damage a restaurant's success, as some apparently have, then there is no certainty that food blogs cannot have the same impact, particularly the ones that enjoy strong and loyal followings.[9] So there is a chance that chefs are not simply being paranoid, as Hayward suggests, but rather that they are acutely aware of this highly unlevel new playing field. Benihana, a Japanese restaurant operating in Kuwait, was certainly of the opinion that a blogger could affect their success when they served a local food blogger with legal papers asking for $18,000 in damages for writing an unfavorable review (Ungerleider 2011). (Then again, seeing as the incident led to a "PR fiasco" for the restaurant, including the formation of a well-liked "Boycott Benihana Kuwait" Facebook page, maybe this restaurant, and people like Jeff Chodorow, ought to have kept their paranoia under wraps.)

Another incident of restaurant fear was intended to damage not a blogger, but S. Irene Virbilia, long-standing restaurant critic for the *Los Angeles Times*, who had managed to stay mostly anonymous for more than fifteen years. While waiting for a table at Red Medicine in Beverly Hills, Virbilia was approached by one of the restaurant's owners and informed that she was not welcome. He then took a picture of her and posted it on their Tumblr site "so that all restaurants can have a picture of her and make a decision as to whether or not they would like to serve her." In the end, that too, according to *L.A. Weekly*'s Jonathan Gold (the first food writer to be recognized with a Pulitzer Prize for criticism), "did no real harm to Virbilia—if anything, they lent her pluckiness—but they made themselves look second-rate" (Gold 2010).

Recognizing the power of established and amateur reviewers alike, some restaurants are taking more innovative social media approaches to dealing with negative criticism. When Eddie Haung's New York restaurant, Xiao Ye, received no stars from Sam Sifton (then the reviewer for the *New York Times*), Huang took the unusual step of conceding on his blog (Fresh Off the Boat) that he had not realized that people "expected more" of him, and that he was going to "change . . . [his] attitude." He also posted a copy of a scolding e-mail his mother had sent to him, comparing his ranking to "The Food Net Work [sic] competition Judge's comments. . . . There is a reason why the other guy won," and concluding that her son should consider returning to his former profession as a lawyer. In his account of the incident, Francis Lam (then of *Salon*, now writing for *Gilt Taste*) wrote that what he found "lovely . . . about this story is that you get the sense that there was a different kind of dynamic here at play than the average restaurateur-critic slamdance. . . . In this case it seems, the critic is playing the role of the wise OG, the tough love brother. You can imagine the wry smile behind the beatdown, the teeth-clenched command to Huang to step yo' game up" (Lam 2010). As another example of making the best of the worst, Boston's Back Bay Social Club has taken to compiling lists of "our top ten favourite not so great reviews" and using them to advertise the restaurant in a way that "deflate[s] the griping though humor," as the *Huffington Post* tells it (Huffington Post 2011a). Samples include sentiments like "they had 'pop slop' music droning on. You know the selection—something for everyone to hate," and "both items were delicious, but let's be honest, you could fry a shoe & i'd love it."

YELP, ZAGAT, AND THE "WISDOM OF CROWDS"

These sorts of reviews are firmly at home in what is possibly the most contentious category of contemporary restaurant "criticism," namely from crowd-sourced sites like Urbanspoon and Yelp. Founded in 2004, Yelp provides "the fun and easy way to find and talk about great (and not so great) local businesses,"[10] which they do by offering up, as their slogan promises, "Real People. Real Reviews." As popular as these "real" reviews are to consumers—at least one survey indicates that while around 14 percent of restaurant goers rely on advice from professional restaurant critics, up to 42 percent prefer user-review websites (Aronica 2011)—"Yelpers," as users of the latter site are known, have fast emerged as the bane of both professional critics and restaurateurs, exemplifying as they do the most democratic of social media platforms, where everyone and anyone really can have a say, regardless of expertise or even motive. Yet, and as one measure of the success of the model, even within the egalitarian parameters of a site like Yelp do hierarchies exist, here in the form of the Yelp Elite Squad. The Squad is made up of members who are recognized and rewarded for "Yelpitude," which includes "reviews that are insightful, engaging and personal (aka useful, funny, and cool!)"; for "Profiles that really sing!"; and for "Personal pizzazz!"[11] Once in the club, Yelp Elites get invited to exclusive events and parties hosted by Yelp, often at restaurants eager to feed people who are eager to write reviews that will get them into restaurants eager to feed people eager to write reviews, and so the cycle goes, while Craig Claiborne presumably turns in his grave.

So goes one version of the story of Yelpers, whose reputation includes being dubbed "foochebags" —a combination of "foodie" and "douchebag" (Norton 2011a)—for engaging in "degenerate feeding frenzies" at Elite events (Forbes 2011a). More generally, Yelpers are notorious for publishing mean-spirited reviews and publishing swiftly, the most memorable of which must be the poor review of chef and *Masterchef* judge Graham Elliot's new restaurant Grahamwich—before it had opened.[12] So Yelpers are, according to at least one chef, "bored, jobless layabouts with not many friends who are convinced that they're going to have a bad time before they even step through the door of a joint" (quoted in Brion 2010). A document to this perspective is the Tumblr site Fuck You Yelper, which aggregates Yelp reviews that fit the site's description as "An Exploration of the Douchebaggery Idiots Commit When Enabled With An Internet Connection, Enough Money For A Meal, And A Sense of Entitlement."[13]

That is only one perspective, and there is another that holds that compilations of consumer reviews on sites like Yelp (which uses a star-rating system) and Urbanspoon (which registers how many users click "I like it" or "I don't" for a restaurant) are more useful—because more representative of "everyman"—than reviews by single experts. At best, this utility generates a positive feedback loop, where other consumers are motivated to post reviews that are (hopefully) "inspiring and engaging," as per the criteria for promotion to Yelp's Elite Squad. Restaurants do pay attention, with several owners taking time to thank reviewers for positive feedback and making apologies for any noted flaws in food or service. For Chris Sommers, owner of Pi pizzeria in St. Louis (who was famously flown to Washington to prepare pizzas for a White House meal in 2009), staying aware of online reviews is something of "an obsession," but with a clear purpose: "We have to embrace the immediacy of Web reviews and social media because they're like what the old customer-comment cards used to be for restaurants. By being an active part of that dialogue on the Web, we can mitigate negative experiences and create positive ones" (quoted in Benn 2010). One Yelper who received personal correspondence from Sommers less than a day after posting a five-star review of Pi, thought the response "was impressive" and made him feel a connection to the restaurant he otherwise wouldn't have (quoted in Benn 2010).

Divergent views on whether Yelpers are helpers or foochebags in the world of restaurants and social media came interestingly to the fore following the news, in September 2011, of Google's acquisition of Zagat, that stalwart of American restaurant criticism since 1979. An early adopter of the philosophy that would later be dubbed "the wisdom of crowds" in James Surowiecki's 2004 book of that name, and that informs crowd-sourced sites like both Yelp and Wikipedia, Zagat has long operated on the premise "that the shared opinions of thousand of avid consumers with real experience are inherently more accurate than the opinions of just one or two critics."[14] However, unlike newer sites, not just anyone gets a voice: historically, Zagat membership comes at a fee (which explains why Google has previously neglected to include Zagat links in restaurant search results), and reviews are edited into "concise, witty quotes" before publication. One commenter noted that Google's acquisition of Zagat represented a paradigm shift for the search engine, whose stated ambition has been to organize the world's information, whereas now it will own content. "All of which makes us think: if Google thought it was buying relevance with the Zagat purchase, it might want to consider enlisting a different demographic of user reviews" (Birdsall 2011a). Implicit here is the suggestion that Zagat's historical business model is essentially outdated. As *Good*'s lifestyle editor Amanda Hess (2011) commented at the time, "a Google-owned Zagat will undoubtedly look a lot Yelpier. And for anyone who values reasoned opinion, that's too bad." But, she predicted, "Yelp's rise made Zagat irrelevant, and so Zagat will become more like Yelp."

Yelp and Zagat are, of course, not the only sites that will help you to decide where to eat. If you are looking for real cheap eats in New York, you can visit Real Cheap Eats NY, a site compiled by two dozen bloggers. Hotspot Robot will help you to find the "best-of-the-best" spots in the city of your choice with its aggregated reviews only from professional critics and recognized publications. There is the proliferation of sites offering special restaurant deals like Groupon, InBundles, BlackBoardEats, and Google Offers. And though he is not, at his own admission, a "critic," if you follow him on Twitter, Josh Ozersky will also tell you where to eat. But the story of Yelp versus Zagat—which may soon not be so different as to merit a "versus"—does well to illustrate the main points of the "everyone is a critic" narrative of this chapter. Despite headlines like "The End of the Career Food Critic" (Martin 2011) following the departure from these posts by Sam Sifton at the *New York Times* and Pat Bruno at the *Chicago Tribune*, the guiding concern is not so much that professional critics will become redundant: in matters of aesthetics it is almost certain that enough people will continue to defer to single experts rather than the crowd—and it may even be the case that, as some established critics have expressed, the crowd helps to keep the professionals on their toes. As Ruth Reichl put it soon after the 2011 James Beard Writing Awards, she did not "know much" when she started writing, but her audience "knew less. Today, this audience is so informed, it makes it really interesting for professional restaurant critics now. They'd better know what they were talking about" (quoted in Fallik 2011).[15]

As Reichl's comments imply, the real story here is less about the professionals versus the amateurs as it is about generalized access to information, where "access" must now be understood in its new "prosumption" hybrid—that is, as both the ability to consume and to produce information. Social media are unprecedented for facilitating this access, but according to Neal Gabler, the instinct is far from novel:

It is certainly no secret that the internet had eroded the authority of traditional critics and substituted Everyman opinion on blogs, websites, even on Facebook and Twitter where one's friends and neighbours can get to sound off. What is less widely acknowledged is just how deeply this populist blowback is embedded in America and how much of American culture has been predicated on a conscious resistance to cultural elites. It is virtually impossible to understand America without understanding the long ongoing battle between cultural commissars who have always attempted to define artistic standards and ordinary Americans who take umbrage at those commissars and their standards. (Gabler 2011a)[16]

Acknowledging that authority is no longer solely in the hands of these so-called cultural commissars, Gabler concludes that "We live, then, in a new age of cultural populism—an age in which everyone is not only entitled to his opinion but is encouraged to share it. Nothing could be more American."

Seen from this perspective, social media as platforms for sharing are the perfect expression of the American psyche, and so is the (possible) Yelpification of Zagat. Equally American—and, of course, not exclusive to Americans—is a distress around particular sorts of sharing. The examples in chapter 2 relating to intellectual property rights are one manifestation of this anxiety. In the "everyone is a critic" narrative, centered as it is around the (perceived, at least) juxtaposition of professionals against amateurs, it takes a curious turn in the sphere of online searches for both restaurants and recipes. Given the competition for attention, here the concern is unsurprisingly about getting found in the virtual haystack. But getting found is less determined by who is an amateur or a professional in the food world as it is by the search engines that make information available to the world, and the main player in this game is Google. When Zagat was still mostly independent (they accepted investments from venture capitalists in 2000), for instance, unless the search was not specific to individual restaurants, their listings were invisible to Google users: Google's way of "punishing" anyone who interferes with making information free for all (Lieber 2010). Once acquired by the search engine, Zagat-listed restaurants could be incorporated into Google Places and Maps. Yelp reviews, on the other hand, were freely available on Google, until the latter was accused of importing those reviews onto its Places pages and not linking back to Yelp (Dignan 2011).

SEARCHING FOR RECIPES: TO GOOGLE OR NOT TO GOOGLE?

So for all the Internet giant's ambitions to liberate the world's information, Google's services have not all been without conflict, and that includes the controversial Google Recipe Search introduced in February 2011. Based on the data that approximately 1 percent of all searches are for recipes (amounting to about 10 million recipe searches a day on Google alone),[17] Recipe Search was intended to circumnavigate any information not classified as a recipe (just as searching through Google Scholar or Google Books would allow a user not to be sent straight to Wikipedia, for example). It was not the first of its kind: Microsoft introduced its Recipes Pages in 2010, allowing Bing users searching for, say, chocolate chip cookies, to choose to go straight to a "recipes task page" (rather than being directed to other information not related to actually baking the cookies), where they could access a number of recipes with the added feature that Bing calculated nutritional information like fat and calorie content against the other search results. Google's features include being able to add or eliminate particular ingredients (like chocolate cake with cherries, but without flour), being able to choose recipes that require less than 15, 30, or 60 minutes, and recipes with less than 100, 200, or 500 calories.

Despite the convenience of choice and access promised by these features, initial reactions to Google Recipe Search were overwhelmingly negative, and particularly from food bloggers. The problem here was first that Google (like Microsoft before it) was mainly linking to recipes from major, established sites like Epicurious, Food Network, and Allrecipes—the "behemoth cooking sites," as Julia Moskin (2011a) calls them—rather than a more democratic (and potentially interesting and useful) selection of results, including from food bloggers. The reason was simple enough: the technological criteria for getting found had changed. Whereas previously most websites, including blog platforms, could use tags and keywords to maximize their search engine optimization (SEO), to be featured in Google Recipes required an additional level of electronic tagging known as metadata, or "rich snippets," to be coded onto requisite categories like cooking times, nutritional information, and photographs. The "real innovation" with this technique, according to Ryan Singel (formerly of *Wired*'s Epicenter),

> is in the background: the entire search is built on structured data that webmasters have built into their webpages using markup code that's invisible to humans but is extremely useful to machines. . . . So for instance, Google is able to show a searcher only Pho recipes that use tofu that take less than a half an hour to make, not by searching for pages that include the word "Pho" and "Tofu" and "Recipe," but by actually knowing that a recipe for something called "Pho" has an ingredient "Tofu" and a listed cooking time of 1 hour. (Singel 2011)

As exciting as this sort of development is for those who predict a semantic Web with sentient-like computers that actually "know" what phở is, it is less exciting for real people like bloggers who are unlikely to have webmasters—like the "behemoth" sites do—to encode their recipes and pictures (at the time of writing, an "hRecipe" plug-in was available on some blog platforms that would create rich snippets, but it was not yet standard). This means that recipes from less technically proficient bloggers—or bloggers who may just not be inclined to pander to Google's technical requirements—will be invisible to anyone using Google Recipe Search. David Lebovitz's response summarizes the sentiments of many who reacted: "I write recipes for readers, not for search engines, and I am being penalized for it" (quoted in Moskin 2011a).

Amanda Hesser highlighted another issue with the Recipe Search when she managed to find a cassoulet recipe featuring both lamb and sausage that would supposedly come in at seventy-seven calories per serving and, as there is no option for choosing a recipe that takes longer than sixty minutes, would presumably take less than one hour to prepare. As she noted, "No such dish exists, unless the serving size is a pinch," not to mention that cassoulet takes at least four hours to make. With its focus on cooking times and calories (presumably as an indicator of "healthiness"), she concludes that Google's Recipe Search does a fundamental disservice to real cooking and instead services the "American eating and cooking disorder":

> The proliferation of cooking times has not only put pressure on writers to fudge times, but has encouraged editors to stop running recipes that take longer than an hour. Lost in the rankings will be such slow-build classics as paella and layer cakes. . . . As it stands, Google's recipe search gives undue advantage to the "quick & easy" recipe sites, encourages dishonesty, and sets up people to be dissuaded from cooking, as they will soon learn that recipes always end up taking more time than they expected. Alas, the search algorithm fundamentally misunderstands what recipe searchers are really looking for: great recipes. (Hesser 2011)

Hesser's summary offers an intriguing turnaround to the "amateurs vs. professionals" narrative of restaurant criticism, where the "behemoths" are the ones under virtual attack from the Yelping masses. Here, by contrast, it is the newer voices—of bloggers, and smaller sites—who are understood as the guardians of real cooking, and who are under threat of the corporate giants otherwise recognized as professionals in the industry of recipe provision.

Fortunately for Hesser and all those who share her views, there is plenty of recipe life beyond Google, just as there remain plenty of single experts to consult instead of Yelp when it comes to choosing a restaurant. Foodily, which you can log onto through Facebook, provides "a continuous feed of recipes that your friends have discovered," and lets you "search and save what you love."[18] Gojee kicks up recipes based on what you crave or have in the pantry (including the possibility of eliminating ingredients you might dislike). If you are in the mood for food and music, visit Drinkify or Turntable Kitchen, where you can find out what tunes best pair with, say, roasted broccoli with anchovy sauce (Elvis Costello's "This Year's Model," according to Turntable Kitchen), or buy the book-CD *The Recipe Project* featuring recipes by top chefs set to music. Food Blog Search is also powered by Google (as is Cookzillas: The Recipe Search Engine) but only returns results from blogs. For Yahoo! users, Food on Shine provides recipes not only from the behemoths, but also from real-food champions like Mark Bittman. Once you have found your favorite recipes, MacGourmet recipe software lets you build and publish your very own cookbook, which you can then sync to your MacGourmet Touch app for iPhone and iPod. Still, looking for an asparagus recipe for a dinner party, Julia Moskin (2011a) found the site Eat Your Books to be the most useful: with no actual recipes, this site indexes listings from cookbooks, magazines, and blogs, making easy the work of searching for recipes that are already in your kitchen library.

For those who prefer watching to reading, YouTube, which was also acquired by Google in 2006 but has so far remained the principal portal for user-generated content, provides as much for the "gastronomically obsessed" (Lindeman 2010) as it does for anyone who is obsessed with cats jumping in and out of cardboard boxes,[19] or pretty much anything else for that matter. In the three years between 2008 and 2011, recipe searches on YouTube quadrupled, while specific search terms like "slow cooking" and "healthy" enjoyed a 5,000 percent increase in just two years (Fahr 2011).[20] Not to confine anyone to their actual computer screens, YouTube is, of course, also available as a mobile phone and tablet computer app(lication), as is the Google+ cooking school, and Taste TV, the "multiplatform vehicle that delivers food, wine, fashion, travel and lifestyle lovers exciting and delicious programming from around the U.S., Canada and the World."[21]

To be sure, apps are arguably the fastest-growing platforms for food and social media, allowing users to consume, to produce, and to be unrestricted in their mobility as they do so. For cooking, this includes the obvious convenience of having someone like Mark Bittman with you in the kitchen to teach you How To Cook Everything (voted the best food app by both *Bon Appetit* and *Toque Magazine* in 2011, and previously the winner of Gizmodo silver), or Martha Stewart guiding you through Smoothies and Cookies (the number 1 paid-for iPad lifestyle app in the summer of 2011). Or using the Epicurious app to compile a shopping list for that dinner party you may be planning. For restaurant goers, it means being able to look up a restaurant on Zagat, find a deal on BlackBoardEats (or on Happy Hours, if cheap drinking is more important than eating) while on the subway, or simply scanning an area with your phone to locate the nearest coffee shop, pizzeria, or food truck (geolocation apps, also known as location-based services [LBS], work with GPS data to find locations close to your own, while "augmented reality" apps provide the added feature of live, 3-D feeds of your physical surroundings). For those who want to see and share pictures, it means being able to log onto Foodspotting to see which foods have been spotted near you that may be worth trying (or avoiding). As Tanya Steel, editor in chief of Epicurious, commented several years ago in the context of the growing number of food websites, "this is one area where millions of people out there cannot learn enough. . . . They cannot eat enough" (quoted in Holahan 2007). Whether this is ultimately good or bad news for those who make it their business to evaluate food remains to be seen. Perhaps the best we can hope for is something to help us evaluate who is worth listening to when it comes to finding both restaurants and recipes. There will surely be an app for that soon enough.

NOTES

1. Bruni did begin his review by invoking Ramsay's "foul mouth and foul temper" TV persona, noting his surprise at finding the restaurant "coolly, even icily, elegant." But there was also mention of "a few off-putting concoctions, like a cloying, gummy wedge of turbot poached in St. Émilion and a bizarre appetizer combining delicate little langoustine tails with indelicate nuggets of boneless chicken wing, crusted with hazelnuts and sweetened with maple syrup. Eric Ripert, meet Colonel Sanders" (Bruni 2007a).

2. For an entertainingly intellectual riposte to a poor review of the food at Hotel Griffou from Sam Sifton (who took the critic's chair at the *New York Times* after Bruni and before moving to the national news desk, and here referred to as ex-reviewer, or "E.R"), see Keyes 2011: "E.R., you were just learning your job after two years. Griffou will stay on; we just turned two, and we know we have a lot to learn. Inspiration from Voltaire, I advise E.R. at the national news desk: may the garden of national news be cultivated in ways that enlighten our perspective, in ways opposite to the dim view you laid down upon Griffou. This retort attempts to master my misery over E.R.'s miserable meanness (from Julius Caesar): 'There is a tide in the affairs of men, which taken at the flood, leads on to fortune; Omitted, all the voyage of their life is bound by shallows and in misery.' May we take this tide, at flood level!"

3. Following a litany of complaints under the heading "Why Does Everyone Hate John Mariani?" in Grub Street Chicago, Mariani posted a rebuttal denying all allegations of not paying for meals and also noted that he has "been characterized wrongly as a 'restaurant reviewer,'" explaining that his official title at *Esquire* is "food and travel correspondent," under which he writes "features, not reviews" (Mariani 2009).

4. According to William Rice (formerly of the *Chicago Tribune*), restaurant reviewing is "the least understood, the least researched, and the most difficult of the critical arts. There are no textbooks. There are no schools. And beyond that, if I review a movie, the people who go the next night are going to see exactly the same performance. But in a restaurant—even on the same night I'm there!—somebody sitting two tables away ordering much the same food could well be having a very different experience" (quoted in Dornenburg and Page 1998, 54).

5. http://www.ftc.gov/os/2009/10/091005endorsementguidesfnnotice.pdf (accessed October 7, 2011).

6. In 2009, Freeman hired lawyers to try to prevent Adam Rucinsky from using her name (both Danyelle Freeman and Restaurant Girl) in tweets and blog posts where he was posing as her. One of his blog posts is titled "It's not free if I don't blog about it" (http://thegourmetglossary.typepad.com/the_gourmet_glossary/2009/08/its-not-free-if-i-dont-blog-about-it-the-redhead.html, accessed October 2, 2011).

7. http://www.behindtheburner.com/expert/danyelle_freeman.html (accessed October 2, 2011).

8. Not directly related to commenting on the establishment, but to restaurants being aware of their customers through their social media activity is *CNN Eatocracy* Kat Kinsman's story of being directed to a restaurant through Twitter recommendations (via the #twitterfeedmehashtag). Not in the mood to make menu decisions (she was to attend a funeral the next day), she

asked the kitchen to choose which meats to include on her charcuterie plate, which they did, and also sent out a dish she had not ordered. Quizzing the waiter, she was told that the chef "saw on Twitter that you were having a rough day, . . . and he's really proud of this dish, sooooo . . . " (Kinsman 2011b).

9. One early case involved a description in the *Sydney Morning Herald* in 2003 of a meal that "jangled like a car crash." The review was ruled as defamatory in June 2007 because the restaurant in question had been forced to close three months later. According to its owner, "customers had been put off by [the reviewer's] words," and not, apparently, by anything to do with the restaurant itself (McMahon 2007).

10. http://www.yelp.com/ (accessed November 15, 2011).

11. http://www.yelp.com/elite (accessed November 15, 2011).

12. At least according to Chef Elliot's Twitter status: https://twitter.com/#!/grahamelliot/status/22665576847 (accessed October 20, 2011).

13. http://fuckyouyelper.tumblr.com/ (accessed November 15, 2011).

14. http://www.zagat.com/about-us (accessed October 30, 2011).

15. Jonathan Gold likewise pointed out that "people are knowledgeable about certain things. You cover a noodle shop and then someone blogs that you think you know noodle shops, but there are 100 you haven't written about. There is this one guy who is a blogger and his specialty is ramen and he really knows everything about it and little beyond it. So it's cool, it puts critics in the middle" (quoted in Fallik 2011).

16. In his South By Southwest talk on "The Twisted Psychology of Bloggers vs. Journalists," Jay Rosen (2011) similarly mentions that he has "always found it fascinating that both bloggers and journalists will use the word 'traditional' in referring to the model of professional journalism that is taught in boot camp J-schools and practiced at, say, The Washington Post. That tradition is about 80 to 90 years old, at most. But our experiment with a free press is 250 years old. . . . For people in the press, bloggers vs. journalists is an elaborate way of staying the same, of refusing to change. . . . A shorter way to say this is: it's *fucking neurotic*" (emphases in the original).

17. For an infographic of the most common recipe searches in the United Kingdom for each month of the year, see Bloor 2011. In January 2012 it was reported that "cake" had replaced "chicken" as the "most searched-for food term [in the UK] thanks to TV baking shows" (Whitelocks 2012).

18. http://www.foodily.com/ (accessed October 25, 2011).

19. Maru the cat is one of the original YouTube memes. By October 2011, videos of Maru (who lives in Japan) had been viewed 100 million times, and a book consisting of "95 glossy pages of photographs of Maru being a cat" was Amazon's best-selling cat-themed book three weeks before its publication (Leith 2011).

20. As an index of YouTube's role in feeding those with an appetite for "gastro-porn," in July 2011, the Canadian-based YouTube channel Epic Meal Time had more subscribers than Justin Bieber (Independent 2011b).

21. http://www.tastetv.com/foodchannel-about.html (accessed July 29, 2011).

Chapter Five

The Business of Pleasure

We have so far seen good evidence of the ways in which social media have empowered consumers to take on tasks previously left (largely) to professionals, such as posting reviews and recipes, and how these activities have in turn had a positive impact on generating virtual communities. Now we turn to more direct ways in which social media benefit professionals, which is to say their growing importance—in some cases indispensability—to food as a commercial enterprise. According to one survey carried out in 2010, 81 percent of participating restaurants were already using social media as marketing platforms (primarily Facebook, which only 3 percent of the surveyed restaurants did *not* use). More than half of those restaurants had observed "more positive mentions as a result of their social-media presence" (Colaizzi 2010). When it comes to patrons, Dawn Sweeney (president of the National Restaurant Association) maintains that "92 percent of social media users eat at a sit-down restaurant at least once a month, 58 percent of Americans now view restaurants online and 16 percent of all consumers are connecting with their favourite restaurants through Facebook, YouTube or MySpace," concluding that social media are indispensable tools for creating "the connection" with consumers (quoted in Liddle 2011). These numbers confirm that the social media phenomenon has rapidly become as important for growing business as it has been for growing pleasure, although in the context of monetizing food experiences—through restaurants, earning a living through food writing or recipe development, and/or building and maintaining a brand as a food celebrity—the collision between business and pleasure that social media facilitate is at once the most obvious and the most ambiguous. [1]

(THE RIGHT KIND OF) ATTENTION IS KEY

It is obvious because of the speed with which platforms like Twitter and Facebook have become central for branding through "friendship," and it is ambiguous for exactly the same reason. Does hitting "like" on the Facebook fanpage of a restaurant or celebrity chef make you their friend or a loyal (virtual) patron? Imagine that you follow Mario Batali or Gordon Ramsay on Twitter and get one of them to acknowledge your request for an acknowledgment—typically a retweet—because it is your birthday (Batali and Ramsay both do this regularly). Is this meaningful or exciting because you are following one of them, or because one of them is (maybe) following you? The answers to both of these scenarios are likely a bit of both, so the questions, being false dichotomies, are not quite fair. These are games of attention with the obvious ideal outcome that someone will cash in on the publicity, but outside of strict monetary measures, it is less clear who is cashing in on what. As *Slate*'s Esther Dyson argues,

> increasingly, individuals go online to get attention, not to give it. Accordingly, companies need to learn how to give customers the attention that they crave, rather than demanding customers' attention and then charging them extra for the attention that their brand commands. . . . Companies are now busily developing metrics for attention: the number of Twitter or Google+ followers or Facebook friends; reputation points for being a good seller, buyer, or reviewer; Klout® scores;[2] game-player status; and so on. Individuals value these scores, but not because they want to buy or sell them (in general, they cannot). They value them in part because they want to draw attention to themselves, from more valuable people. But, in part, they just value the status itself. (Dyson 2011)

What we see, then, is not a turnaround per se, but rather an intriguing readjustment of the traditional business model that operates with the simple goal of generating customers through brand attention. That goal still holds, but now brand attention is increasingly premised on giving some of that attention back to the consumer. In the spirit of social media, transactions have become more conversational, reciprocal, and "fun." But for all the clear opportunities of social media branding, the "friendly" relationships are paradoxically also more tenuous, as bad publicity has as strong a chance of going viral as do the "positive mentions."

Take the example of ConAgra's misguided efforts to use bloggers to generate positive publicity. As we have seen with restaurants and individual chefs paying attention to what bloggers (and Yelpers) are saying about them, so too has the food industry recognized the power of bloggers as a guiding force of "socialnomics," namely the principle that "You can't just say it. You have to get the people to say it to each other" (Qualman 2009). So it was that in August 2011, a number of food and "mom" bloggers were invited to "an intimate Italian restaurant" in New York for a "delicious four-course meal," supposedly prepared by Food Network chef George Duran. They were further told that on confirmation of attendance, they would each receive an extra pair of tickets that they could give away to readers, as well as an "unexpected surprise." The surprise turned out to be the food they were served, which was not cooked by Duran, but rather, for the main course, a previously frozen Marie Callender's (one of ConAgra's brands) Three Meat and Four Cheese Lasagna, and for dessert, Marie Callender's Razzleberry Pie. There were also hidden cameras in the venue to record people's reactions to the food, apparently intended for use as online promotional material (Newman 2011).

What the organizers of the event (the PR and marketing firm Ketchum, which ConAgra had hired to coordinate the event) had not anticipated was the almost uniform reaction of anger and irritation at discovering what they were eating. One particularly unhappy blogger, host of Mom Confessionals (a blog that boasts badges from Theta Mom Community, BravadoMama Ambassador, and Blog with Integrity, among others), wrote that the "entire meal was a *SHAM!*," and that she was deeply embarrassed at having wasted both her husband's time (he accompanied her to the event for a rare occasion of an evening together without their children) and that of her children's pediatrician and his wife, who had won the extra set of tickets (Chan 2011). Besides the false premises of getting them to the event, other attendees were annoyed at having been "tricked" into consuming a meal that they would never consciously choose because it was either "chemical-filled" or "loaded with sodium." Following these negative comments, which also made their way onto Facebook and Twitter, ConAgra canceled the last of the five planned events, publicly apologized for putting "any bloggers or their guests in an uncomfortable position," and offered to recompense them for any travel and babysitting costs incurred. So this was one example that disproved the assumption that bloggers (at least these ones) are willing to do anything for a free meal—or for an offer of $20, which professional chef and cookbook author Virginia Willis declined from an unnamed fast-casual restaurant to promote its "value offers" on her site (Willis 2011)—and shows that the food industry undermines that assumption at their own peril. As Deborah Silverman, head of the Board of Ethics and Professional Standard at the Public Relations Society of America, commented of the event, even though "Ketchum has an excellent reputation for high ethical standards, . . . the social media realm (including bloggers) is new territory for public relations practitioners, and I view this as a valuable learning opportunity" (quoted in Newman 2011).

One industry giant that has taken good notice of this new territory is McDonald's, which for several years has nurtured a unit of "Mom's Quality Correspondents" to blog about visits to suppliers and so on in an effort to convince other moms to support the fast-food chain's stated commitment to more healthful and sustainable practices. The director of social media for McDonald's explained the strategy as recognizing that "Mom bloggers are very networked and very linked-in. They spread information very, very quickly." Most importantly, "Moms listen to other moms more than they listen to other folks" (quoted in Kinsman 2011a). Taking advantage of this power of moms to direct the—hopefully positive—attention of other moms to their brand, McDonald's has made a point of forging a presence at important blogging events like BlogHer 2010, which coincided with the nationwide launch of its new oatmeal, and throughout which it was active on Twitter using the conference's #BlogHer10 hashtag. In 2011, with plans to revamp its Happy Meals to include healthier options, mom bloggers were again asked for their input—and subsequent social media output. Reactions from the "mom-o-sphere," as *CNN Eatocracy*'s Kat Kinsman (2011a) dubs it, were unsurprisingly mixed, the range of which perhaps is best captured in the titular question of one post on Blogher: "McDonald's Happy Meal: PR Stunt or Health Win?"

Ambiguous attitudes to the involvement of "big industry" in turning around a food environment that is typically qualified as "toxic" or "unhealthy"—thanks largely to the original successes of major corporations like McDonald's and ConAgra with their "chemical-filled," sodium- and saturated fat-laden options—is to some extent understandable. It also runs the risk of unduly pigeonholing the motives of anyone whose main aim is to generate profit. The historical rift is generally determined by size: big corporations are not to be trusted, while smaller concerns—including single individuals—are more personal and personable, and therefore more genuine. With the advent of social media, it becomes more difficult to trust that particular script (notwithstanding that it may not have been a useful rule of thumb in the first place). Which is simply to say: how are we, as consumers, to know that McDonald's motives for gaining a social media presence through moms represents anything more sinister than Mario Batali's motives for interacting with his fans on Twitter? Or, to ask a different question, is it not possible that the blog post title quoted above offers us another false choice, and that McDonald's is engaging in a strategy that is *both* a PR stunt and a health win because it recognizes that without the support of social media tastemakers its brand is in possible jeopardy? While their food offerings are radically different, McDonald's and Mario Batali do share a business goal, which is to sell as much of their product as possible. For a public figure like Batali, this includes the requirement to at times *act* as that public figure—meaning to get into his television character—rather than himself, so as not to disappoint fans.[3]

This is not intended as an endorsement of either McDonald's or of Mario Batali (even if personal preferences would lead this writer to a Batali restaurant in an instant, and to a McDonald's more like never). It is only to point out that whether talking about major corporations, individual celebrities, or even ordinary individuals, the social media activities we engage in are all potentially subject to the same sorts of queries about motives and authenticity. Can we claim to be 100 percent genuine, for instance, if we are only prompted to remember a friend's birthday thanks to Facebook? What if the recipient of our "best wishes" is not really a friend, but a "friend": someone whom we have not met for decades and perhaps never really were friendly with when we were in physical proximity? For the most part, social networking allows us not to have to confront these questions, or at least not to take them too seriously. This is at least partly due to the restrictions of time and attention that most of us face, and that is no less true when it comes to people who use—and consume—social media dedicated to promoting the business of pleasure. Where there is actual evidence that McDonald's is engaging in dishonest and/or misleading behavior that could pose harms to people's health, then, of course, they must be scrutinized, and at best exposed for such.[4] Until such time, questioning their motives is likely to be as fruitful as wondering whether Gordon Ramsay *really* thinks the cake you tweeted him a picture of is "stunning," or whether Mario Batali actually enjoys answering any- and everyone's questions about his favorite places to eat in particular cities (even if the latter did tweet "LOVE" in answer to a Twitter follower's question of, "Why do you waste your precious tweets on question easily answered with a little research on the 'net?" November 21, 2011).

If the volume of Batali's social media output is any gauge, then he certainly does appear to enjoy it. He regularly "checks in" and unlocks badges at restaurants with Foursquare, which also allows him to share pictures with Twitter and Foursquare followers of what he is eating at any given moment.[5] The chef has also officially partnered with Foursquare to provide special deals at his more than a dozen restaurants across New York, Las Vegas, and Los Angeles. In addition to discounted food, users who check in at one of the restaurants can unlock a Batali badge, the social value of which is presumably determined by how exciting it is to own a virtual Batali-branded badge, or more plausibly by communicating to your own followers that you have eaten at a Batali restaurant. As the *Huffington Post* reported it, the "partnership makes sense for the location-based social network. According to recent data, 'food' was the most popular check-in category among Foursquare users in 2010" (C. Smith 2011). To be sure, geolocation apps have become increasingly popular in recent years, with Foursquare (launched in 2009) itself boasting around seven million users worldwide (Gowalla and Placepop are rival apps, while Facebook and Google also allow users to "check in" to announce their locations to friends and followers). More to the point of capitalizing on this new penchant for broadcasting not only our thoughts but our whereabouts, more and more restaurants (just some of the 25 million merchants registered with Foursquare) are registering with the site to offer users special rewards, such as discounts or freebies, like a cookie at Whole Foods, free appetizers at Chili's, and mozzarella sticks at Applebee's if you check in with more than one person (Independent 2011a). These are corollaries to other social media perks such as signing up for a restaurant's Facebook fanpage in order to get coupons for admission to "exclusive" Facebook parties, including a free snack and a margarita, as Besito Mexican restaurant in Huntington, New York, offers (DiCarlo 2011).

These are innovative and inexpensive ways to get "butts on seats," which is after all the main aim of any restaurant. As an index of how indispensable social media is becoming to fulfilling this aim is the Restaurant Social Media Index (RSMI), a joint effort between Nation's Restaurant News and analytics firm DigitalCoCo "developed to provide learning that will help restaurants become more robust and effective in the use of social media, digital content and brand development."[6] The RSMI is useful not only for established businesses to compare themselves to their competition—in November 2011 Starbucks had the highest RSMI score, or "social footprint," followed by Wendy's, Chick-fil-A, McDonald's, and Outback Steakhouse—but also for newcomers to get a sense of what the playing field looks like (the RSMI website features a live feed of the top ten brands on Twitter, for example, making it possible to track real-time conversations between restaurants and customers). Once seats are filled, there are a number of other social media innovations designed to keep people there for longer than they may otherwise have stayed. Tested with positive initial results in Boston, TextMy-Food™ allows patrons to text additions to their orders when their server is not immediately available: "By making it easier and even fun to order that second round and additional appetizers, guests order more at the restaurant where the system is in use" (RestaurantNews 2010). Developed by a former MIT student in the Bay Area, the E La Carte system lets diners use touch screen tablets to place their orders, play games while they wait, and pay online, including splitting checks. With competition from Dallas-based Ziosk, Microsoft's Surface technology and the increasing amount of restaurants using iPads in place of menus (Pepitone 2011), this form of interactive service may be in its relative infancy but is likely to become more common in the not-so-distant future.[7]

So too, conceivably, is a general improvement of restaurant websites, which *Slate*'s technology columnist Farhad Manjoo characterizes as being for the most part "horrifically bad" (he is not alone, as the Tumblr site, Never Said About Restaurant Sites, humorously demonstrates). It is not because of lack of money or attention—Manjoo muses that certain "food purveyors appear to have spent a great deal of money and time to uglify their pages"—

but rather because a number of restaurateurs still have not acknowledged the importance of the Web and social media to their business in an era where, according to the head of consumer marketing at the online reservation site OpenTable, up to one-third of reservations happen online, and more than 10 percent of patrons "are coming from mobile devices" (Manjoo 2011b). Fast becoming more common is the Web's increasing function as a platform for exposing poor behavior (some examples of which are already chronicled in the cases of "culinary plagiarism" in chapter 2). When one regular user of OpenTable neglected to honor her reservation at a Batali restaurant in Las Vegas, for instance, she received an e-mail from the reservation site informing her that her account had been "suspended due to an excessive accumulation of 'no shows,' per OpenTable policy." This is less remarkable than the fact that the incident was exposed by a friend of the "offender" who writes "Tourist Trap," a weekly Culture Blog at the *San Francisco Chronicle*. Commenting on how troubled relationships ideally find one partner confronting the other before ending it, she concluded:

> Let Tara's plight be a cautionary tale, OpenTable users. It might seem like no big deal to you. You scheduled a date, you thought it was casual and you blew it off. But OpenTable doesn't see it that way. OpenTable is pacing back and forth, candles lit, food getting cold. They've had it! OpenTable deserves better! There is someone out there who will honor this relationship, someone to whom a 1000-point reservation *means* something. The next thing *you* know, reservation flake, you've been dumped by an app. (Spotswood 2011, emphases in the original)

Undoubtedly intended as satire, the post nevertheless provides a useful reminder of the swiftness with which the Web and its accessories—in this case services provided through mobile applications—have become a "friend" to those who play nice and a potential adversary to those who do not.

What often remains ambiguous, though, is who the real "baddie" is in situations like these. In one response to the OpenTable incident, *Chow*'s Joyce Slayton takes the opposite perspective and commends OpenTable "for providing the tiniest nudge to those who need to bone up on their social obligations. Tara can always register from a new email account and you won't be the wiser. But maybe she will" (Slayton 2011). Then there was the incident reported in October 2011, in which a waitress posted a picture on Facebook of a receipt from a recent transaction that had earned her no tip, and a note scribbled by her customer: "P.S. You could stand to loose [sic] a few pounds." These are the sorts of images (generally minus quips about weight) that are regularly posted on sites like 15 Percent, subtitled "A Bunch of Shitty Tips," and accounts of which populate Bitterwaitress and Lousy-Tippers, the latter of which provides the space to "complain to the world and expose those who take advantage of your work,"[8] and also features a "Lousy

Tipper Database" with names of offending customers. In this case, the exposure went further than being listed on a database: thanks to the customer having paid with a credit card, friends of the offended waitress found the man's full name and address and posted his details on Facebook, with the caution that if people do not want to be exposed, "DON'T GIVE THE BARTENDER YOUR CREDIT CARD. We live in a social networking hub." However justified their motives may or may not have been, unfortunately for the waitress, her friends' sleuthing work resulted in exposing details about the wrong man, so she was forced to add an apology on Facebook stating that she "could not be more sorry for posting the wrong person's info and photo. It got a little out of hand, Let's all get Tacos and Happy Hour drinks, and tip 20%!!" (quoted in Chou 2011).

INA GARTEN, ALTON BROWN, AND THE HARSHNESS OF CROWDS

In contrast to the so-called wisdom of crowds, incidents like these, which end up "getting out of hand," are among newer examples of what social psychologists call "deindividuation," or how the so-called mob mentality—that is, acting in a group rather than alone—encourages individuals to behave differently, often in a way that transgresses their personal moral codes by choosing behavior that is more aggressive, destructive, and essentially antisocial.[9] Fortunately this example is relatively mild, and hopefully it incurred no actual harm to the man who was falsely identified as being a perpetrator. But for people whose livelihood depends on their public profiles (and therefore on maintaining a good-natured relationship with fans and customers), the effects of being ganged up on by a virtual crowd can be more disturbing. Consider the case of the "Barefoot Contessa" Ina Garten, who came under fire in March 2011 for allegedly refusing to honor the request (through the Make-A-Wish Foundation) of Enzo, a young fan and cancer patient whose first wish was to cook with his idol. It was not the first time the family had made the request. They had been turned down once before on account of Garten's busy schedule (she had a book tour planned), but when the Foundation approached Garten's representatives a second time, they were given a "definite no," as the boy's mother described it on her blog. There she tells the emotive story of her son's response ("why doesn't she want to meet me?"), and thanks her readers for "all the passion" that drove the "many boycotts . . . and emails, letters, texts" following the news. She does, however, hope that "instead of anger about this situation that we can all just look around and figure out what we can do to make something easier, more peaceful or beautiful for someone else. . . . Ina's mind has been made up and I TRULY feel that it is HER loss" (Mama Pereda 2011a).

If it was not already, it did turn out to be something of a loss for Garten as the mediasphere erupted into judgment of the "Heartless Contessa," or the "Baresoul Cuntessa," as well as a "Get Ina to grant Enzo's wish" Facebook Page and a *Business Insider* article positing that if Garten has time to cook a charity lunch for well-heeled people in the Hamptons, then "she can make time to whip up some meringues with a six-year old" (Angelo 2011). Eventually the boy's mother posted on her blog asking everyone to "PLEASE STOP THE MADNESS," where she also noted her displeasure at her son's media characterization as "poor boy" and "this sick child," pointing out that "NONE of these things describe the boy I live with" (Mama Pereda 2011b). But as media sensationalism goes, this is the kind of hyperbole that helps to validate slandering the "villain," especially in situations where the villainizing is in fact unmerited, as it turned out to be in Garten's case. According to the *Los Angeles Times*'s report on the incident, Garten was "completely blindsided by the media firestorm," the "definite no" that her representatives had given the family were "unbeknown to her," and once aware of the request, she decided to honor the boy's wish after all (Lynch 2011b). Yet as James Norton summarized it in an article on "The High-Tech Smearing of Ina Garten" (and echoing the caution not to "piss off the Internet" we saw in chapter 2), "while the viciousness was no doubt fun while it lasted, it's unlikely that Garten's sympathetic response (and generous offer to meet the boy) will completely fix the problem—when the Internet opens fire on your reputation, the wounds tend to take a long time to heal" (Norton 2011b).

While Garten's livelihood may not have suffered directly from the incident, there is some evidence of the truth of Norton's predictions, at least in terms of how some people take an apparent pleasure in furthering smear campaigns even after the "firestorm" has mostly settled. Writing for the *Philadelphia Inquirer*, "teacher-turned-talk-show-host" Dom Giordano continued the hyperbole as he told his readers about Garten's "halfhearted" offer, adding that the family had declined it, "saying they didn't want to expose their son to more heartbreak" (Giordano 2011), when according to another report Enzo's father had told ABC that they were not going to do it because he did not want his son to go "through any other stress" (quoted in Marikar 2011). In something of a nonsequitur, Giordano also conjectured that "perhaps the fact that Garten doesn't have children of her own prevents her from having compassion for Enzo's simple request." Steadfast in his denial of the possibility that Garten in fact knew nothing of the request, Giordano makes his wider point about her "cold attitude":

With regrets to Charles Barkely [sic; the former professional basketball player who famously stated that sports players should not be considered role models], yes, celebrities are role models. If your paycheck comes from the dollars of the public who watch your shows, buy your books and support the advertisers on your program, there's a minimum obligation to acknowledge your public. Even if Garten was inundated with requests, as her people claimed (and I find hard to believe), I think a wish from a 6-year-old with leukemia deserves special consideration. (Giordano 2011)

He concludes with the note that many of his callers had agreed to put pressure on the Food Network and advertisers to cancel her show, hoping finally (in a rhetorical flourish) that "this is one wish that gets granted."

This example is interesting for the light it sheds on some of the paradoxes of food and social media, where the new virtual proximity of stars to their fans makes them that much easier to reach, and so entrenches a perceived obligation to public responsibility—in this scenario, Garten no longer has the right to say no—and at the same time disallows them the fallibilities of ordinary busy human beings, as Garten has no right *not* to have known about the request in the first place. What is particularly characteristic of the social media climate is that one person's opinion can so easily gain so much traction—even if that opinion misses the crucial bridge into "fact" by having some evidence to back it up. Yet, as Sam Harris put in *The Moral Landscape*, "truth has nothing, in principle, to do with consensus: one person can be right, and everyone else can be wrong. Consensus is a guise to discovering what is going on in the world, but that is all that it is. Its presence or absence in no way constrains what may or may not be true" (Harris 2010, 31). It is, manifestly, another characteristic of the Web that "everyone" can refer to a relatively small group of people: in this instance those readers and listeners who are sympathetic to Giordano's point of view (and the similar views of those who enjoyed punning on Garten's stage name at her expense). If those views are wrong, then we can hope for Garten's sake that they will be or have been corrected by the publication of more balanced reports. Yet in terms of consensus as an index of "what is going on in the world," smear campaigns such as these do little if not provide evidence of the potential nastiness of the virtual crowd.

It is also noteworthy that when it comes to conversations around celebrities and their supposed responsibility to their fans, there is a relative absence of talk about the responsibility of those fans to their idols. This is a subject that Alton Brown (judge of *The Next Iron Chef* and host of Food Network's *Good Eats*) brought to the fore when he deleted his Twitter account in 2011, after someone—"a parasitic troll" in his words—started a fake Twitter account (@DeAnnaBrownEats) posing as his wife, and using a picture of the Brown family as the avatar. After telling @DeAnnaBrownEats on

Twitter that "I'm going to leave twitter to sick, low life scumbags like you. It's all yours, you psychopath" (quoted in Brion 2011), he explained his decision on his blog:

> The way I see it, Twitter is like a big cocktail party. If I was at a cocktail party and someone puked on my wife's shoes, odds are excellent that we'd leave. Does that mean I won't attend any more cocktail parties? Maybe not. Maybe I'll just have to figure out a way to host my own cocktail parties where people actually have to be accountable for their behavior. (Brown 2011a)

However, by the end of the month he posted that "it turns out the sick, lowlife scumbag population on Twitter is actually rather low while the number of nice, normal (seemingly at least) folks is relatively high," so he would be back, but "rest assured . . . I'm loaded for troll" (Brown 2011b). (Being "loaded for troll" presumably included a decision to retweet a number of nasty tweets directed at him, like @evilpeacemaker's, "Hey alton brown? YOU ANNOY THE SHITOUT OFME," or @missAnon011's, "Good eats is the DUMBEST show. Alton brown is soooo annoying," both retweeted on November 11, 2011.)

The incident did presumably get him thinking about his relationship with fans, as he soon thereafter posted his "Fanifesto" in anticipation of an imminent book tour. "Once upon a time," it begins, "fans knew what to expect from the fan/celebrity relationship," which included joining a fan club, buying magazine, or hoping for a glimpse at a gig among thousands of people. He suggest that stars like George Clooney might still fit this model, whereas people like himself belong to an

> ever widening, Warholian spiral of quasi-celebrity. We are the cable-ebrities and the web-ebrities, and unlike the Liz and Dicks of the world, we live, work, eat, shop, worship, and recreate right alongside the rest of you. . . . We wait in lines, drop off the dry cleaning, and interact regularly with the "citizens" around us (that's celebrity-speak for non-famous folk). This situation often stretches the very fabric of our society because we just don't have rules for this sort of thing. (Brown 2011c)

So the Fanifesto comprises Brown's own rules for this "sort of thing," including that fans may not take pictures of his family ("I will go freakin' ballistic"), that he will not sign anything live, or tolerate being approached in a public restroom, that fans on social media should not get offended at being "snubbed," that in person they should behave as fans, not fanatics ("I don't owe you a darned thing"), and finally, that "when it's over, it's over."

For someone who is a self-named "cable-" or "web-ebrity," that is, not a "real" celebrity, it could be considered overkill to draw up this kind of manifesto. But on the assumption that most of these rules are inspired by people having overstepped Brown's personal boundaries in the past, they are also an index of the extent to which social media have helped to intensify the celebrity-generating machine that was, not so long ago, generally the province of more traditional media platforms like television. Indeed, several of Brown's colleagues in the professional food world have "been really positive about the social contract, and some have even asked to borrow and modify it for their own use," while just a "small percentage of the public has been really angry, and to those he says 'stay away'" (E. Smith 2011).

CHEFS AND SOCIAL MEDIA: FOR YOUR EYES ONLY

The discomfort experienced in cases like Garten's or Brown's notwithstanding, for the most part the social mediasphere has been an undeniable boost for people in the business of providing pleasure through food. Many of those food professionals appear not to share Brown's inhibitions about approaching, and even crossing, the virtual line between publicity and privacy. For example, Anthony Bourdain, also an avid Twitter user (where he regularly shares photographs of himself and/or food on shoots), posted a picture of himself and his wife on the red carpet outside the television Emmys in 2011. He wore a tuxedo and his wife wore a long black dress; they both look appropriately chic. They did not look so chic when, the next day, he posted the "after" picture with his wife slumped on his shoulder and both of them looking decidedly worse for wear. There is an obvious argument that points out the difference between someone posting something "private" about themselves, as Bourdain did, and someone else taking an unauthorized picture of their family, which would cause Alton Brown to go "freakin' ballistic." Daniel Solove (2004, 43) provides one plausible summary of this difference: "What people demand when they demand privacy with regard to their personal information is the ability to ensure that the information about them will be used only for the purposes they desire." Of course once posted, Bourdain has no real control over what his picture might be used for—his followers could choose to disregard the copyright terms and conditions of the various sites dedicated to sharing photographs (like Yfrog, Twitpic, or Instagram). Even if it were reproduced without permission on a blog, for example, at least the existence of the picture would come as no surprise to the people depicted in it. [10]

Bourdain is just one of a number of chefs who act as their own paparazzi, regularly posting pictures of themselves on Twitter, even if others like Jamie Oliver and Gordon Ramsay generally avoid images of themselves in compromised states. Of social networking tools, Twitter appears (so far) to be the most versatile: as we have seen, Jamie Oliver also uses the platform to spread news about his #foodrevolution and other latest ventures, including the opportunity to be featured in his magazine ("Ask @jamieoliver your food and cooking questions &he'll answer the best ones in his mag! Include #askJamieO"; October 30, 2011) to attend Twitter parties and to take part in "competwitions." Followers of Wolfgang Puck (@WolfgangBuzz) are treated to new and ongoing specials ("Today! We kick off the two special menus at Lupo in Las Vegas in honor of the King of Pop [& The IMMORTAL tour]," December 5, 2011) as well as asked to help vote for one of his restaurants in the running for an award, as he did when his restaurant The Source was in competition for Washington, DC, Restaurant of the Year in 2011. If you are a fan of baking guru Dorie Greenspan, you could be one of the people who responds to questions such as, "When a recipe says beat a batter in a mixer for 10 full mins, do you follow the directions? Or do you just give it 3 min and call it quits?"(August 11, 2011), which may help her to decide what sorts of instructions to include in her next cookbook.

Reporting on the trend of chefs and social media in the *Wall Street Journal*, Alina Dizik (2011) concludes that whether foodies are looking for actual live engagement or just to be a "fly-on-the-wall, reading others' quick exchanges with the chef . . . Twitter seems to create a sense of personal loyalty between a chef and customers."[11] Although loyal relationships between chefs and customers are hardly new phenomena, social media seem to be increasingly requisite for the relationship: Dizik tells the story of a Chicago chef who decided to leave Twitter and Facebook for a few months. He announced his departure on Twitter, leaving his telephone number and e-mail address so people could still reach him. Not one person did. So he rejoined, arguing that it "is a good way to fill up last minute reservations."

Not all social media action is about getting "butts on seats" or even driving cookbook sales, though. Eddy Huang, whose Fresh Off the Boat blog earned him recognition for "Chefs Using Social Media" in *Chow*'s 13 in 2011 (its third annual awards dedicated to honoring "people pushing the food world in new and adventurous directions"), uses the space to write about being Asian in America "with a street-level take on New York's food life," as *Chow* describes it, which Huang believes addresses a void:

> There is definitely a lack of this content out there. All these downtown kids, people on the street: Dudes are like, "Yo, I read your blog." I'm trying to mobilize those people. A lot of us don't read food writing. Why would we listen to some person who didn't grow up eating Puerto Rican food write about lechonera? That kind of writing is almost for outsiders and tourists, like, restaurant tourists who live in the city, cultural tourists. (quoted in Birdsall 2011b)

Mobilizing a targeted group, as in "those people," is, in the end, an apt way to summarize the business of food and social media. It is a landscape that is already so vast and growing so quickly that it is impossible to characterize in broad strokes. This is because every new turn it takes is designed to capture some segment of the market that may not already be served, or to enhance the experience of an already-existing consumer base that could be served better. Huang's success is based on reaching some of those who eschew "mainstream" food writing, even as it is questionable whether such a thing exists, premised as much of food writing and blogging precisely is on being unique and communicating in a voice that is unlike the other voices. But it is true that the idea of food writing is becoming mainstream in the sense of now being recognized as a possible career choice that interested candidates can study at universities like NYU or take classes on from recognized professionals like Molly O'Neill, whose online courses at Cook 'n' Scribble are "designed to provide you the training and the mentoring that today's freelance food bloggers, authors and writers find tough to come by." [12] For those bloggers and/or food writers who might be confused about whether Chinese cabbage should be written as bokchoy or pakchoi, as of May 2011, the AP Stylebook similarly contains a section on "Food Guidelines" (Hirsch 2011).

In addition to Foursquare deals and innovative ordering technology, more and more restaurants are also using the Web to enhance the experience of regular diners by recording information about their preferences. According to one restaurant owner in Brisbane, Australia, who admits to Googling customers to learn about their backgrounds, the practice "is not so we can spam them every five minutes—it's a question of knowing exactly what they want so that when they do come in we know what their favourite Scotch is, how much soda they take with it, what the lady's favourite Champagne or wine [is] or what she had [at her] last meal" (quoted in Hurst 2011, insertions in the original). The reservations site OpenTable provides storage space for exactly the purpose of restaurants keeping "comment cards" about customers. As John Mariani notes, the only novel thing about this practice is the "high-tech files": top-end restaurants have been keeping notes about customers for a very long time. Yet the technology that makes it easier to do so— and to include the added results of a Google search—also make it easier for more casual restaurants to operate with the personalized service that only the "private clubs" of the past did, especially as one restaurateur suggested, "many of them functions [sic] like private clubs anyway" (Mariani 2011).

It is quite possibly the fact of functioning like private clubs that make social media platforms so lucrative, even if they are "private" only in the sense of requiring membership, which more often than not means simply by pledging attention through Twitter, Facebook, Foursquare, and so on. Jamie Oliver's competwitions are for his Twitter followers—but anyone is welcome to follow him. Similarly, followers—or rather "Twitter followers only"—of Grub Street New York, *New York Magazine*'s food site, are privy to special offers and competitions. In November 2011, *CHOW* issued the challenge to "Like Us, and You Could Have a Reason to Really Like Us": by "Liking" *CHOW*'s Secret Smartphone page on Facebook, fans stood a chance of winning a smartphone loaded with the *CHOW* Thanksgiving Coach app. Launched in April 2010, Opensky.com is "a social shopping venture that pairs food-loving consumers with exclusive access to products promoted by celebrity tastemakers" (the latter including the likes of Michael Ruhlman and Masterchef winner Whitney Miller), giving subscribers the opportunity to "Shop Like a Chef" (Aronica 2010). For those who also like to be in the virtual company of chefs when choosing where to eat, the Chef's Feed iPhone app "lets pros do the yelping" (Dean 2011).

What these examples have in common is a promise of exclusivity. They offer the chance to mingle with the pros or to gain an object or an experience thanks to being one of "those people" who are then rewarded for having done well in choosing where to pay their attention. That said, some offers are, in appearance at least, more exclusive than others, such as Lexus partnering with chefs like Morimoto, Michael Symon, "and four other prime-time gods of cuisine" to offer recipes to Lexus owners. As Lexus pledges on its website, when asked at a dinner party, "So where did you get the recipe?," Lexus drivers get to tell their guests, "You know Chef Morimoto from *Iron Chef America?* He gave it to me." Except that is not quite true. Morimoto might have given it to Lexus, but he also gave it to all the non-Lexus drivers who click on the website, where the recipe for "Masaharu Morimoto's Shiso Stuffed Squid with Squid Ink Gnocchi & Cured Lemon" is available to all, and where readers are encouraged to "try it out and tell us how things went via Facebook and Twitter."[13] Still, Morimoto in this way helps to drive traffic to Lexus, and perhaps some small percentage of that traffic will translate into new Lexus owners who enjoy the "exclusivity" of what the brand has to offer.

It remains too early to say whether social media can overturn the historical driver for exclusivity, which is to say the economic disparities that create actual private clubs, or simply a world of pleasure that only a small minority can afford. This inequality is among the concerns of the Occupy Wall Street (OWS) movement, which began in New York in September 2011, and which has named that minority the "1 percent," as against the "99 percent" majority. Speaking on a *Time* "Person of the Year" panel that November, Mario Batali ventured a comparison between bankers—who in the eyes of the occupiers belong to the villainous "1%"—and Hitler and Stalin. He qualified by explaining that "they're not heroes, but they are people that had a really huge effect on the way the world is operating" (quoted in Bercovici 2011). Batali's comments quickly went viral, with bankers—apparently among Batali's best customers at his high-end New York eateries—allegedly cancelling their reservations and vowing never to set foot in one of his restaurants again (Frank 2011). Or, according to *Eater*'s coverage of the incident, "Mario Batali, chef and member of the 1%, is now pissing off the Wall Street moneybags by calling them as bad as Hitler and Stalin. . . . Yeah, probably the bankers not [sic] going to like that much. Particularly the ones who eat at Batali's upscale New York restaurants, Babbo and Del Posto. Oops" (Forbes 2011b).

The incident cannot have been pleasant for Batali, particularly with Twitter hashtags like #boycottbatali and #bataligate trending on the site where the chef otherwise has a very positive presence, and where he eventually did tweet an apology. In the world of business, there is always someone ready to take advantage of a negative situation; for example, one Goldman employee who told the *Wall Street Journal* that "if fewer bankers go to Babbo, maybe I can finally get a reservation" (quoted in Frank 2011). So it is likely that Batali will not suffer in the long run. Still, there may be a cautionary tale to take away from stories like this one, the one involving Ina Garten, and the numerous others featured in this chapter. It is clear that social media are helping to redefine best business practice as one that involves an enormous amount of attention. To be sure, in the social mediasphere, attention is capital. But attention spans are also limited by competing interests, which means that actions and words can be as quickly misrepresented and misunderstood as they can propel someone to overnight fame. Considering today's fickle audience, then, best business practice may be as simple as best behavior: when all actions are on display, none will go unnoticed; and more so than ever before in the business of pleasure, the bottom line depends on who your friends are.

NOTES

1. As Adam Roberts of Amateur Gourmet puts it in his guide on "How To Support Yourself As A Food Blogger" (2011), "Many of your favorite food bloggers (I won't name names) make it seem like they're food blogging for pleasure, but behind-the-scenes they're checking their numbers and statistics the way that a trader checks his or her stock portfolio."

2. A Klout score "measures influence based on your ability to drive action," including your "True Reach" ("How many people you influence"), "Amplification" ("How much you influence them"), and "Network Impact" ("The influence of your network") (http://klout.com/corp/kscore, accessed November 12, 2011). Not everyone agrees that Klout serves an actual utility: "Aside from the occasional quid pro quo freebie, it seems that what Klout exists to do is create status anxiety — to saddle you with a popularity ranking, and then make you feel insecure about it and whether you'll lose that ranking unless you engage in certain activities that aren't necessarily in your interest, but are in Klout's. In other words Klout exists to turn the entire Internet into a high school cafeteria, in which everyone is defined by the table at which they sit. And there you are, standing in the middle of the room with your lunch tray, looking for

a seat, hoping to ingratiate yourself with the cool kids, trying desperately not to get funneled to the table in the corner where the kids with scoliosis braces and D&D manuals sit" (Scalzi 2011).

3. Bill Buford (2006, 158) tells the story of Batali being "spotted on the street, stopped by two guys who recognized him from television, immediately falling in the 'Hey, dude, wow, it's, like, that guy from the Food thing' routine, and Mario, flattered, had thanked them courteously, and they were so disappointed— 'crushed'—that he now travels with a repertoire of quick jokes so as to be, always, in character."

4. It bears noting that at the time of writing, McDonald's was under new fire following the re-release of its notorious McRib sandwich and the release of a video showing that Smithfield's, its pork supplier, was in the practice of using gestation crates for its sows, now generally recognized as inhumane treatment—this despite McDonald's stated commitment to humane and sustainable animal husbandry (McWilliams 2011).

5. Badges refer to various Foursquare status markers. Some are generic, for instance, "newbie" (your first check-in), "adventurer" (after checking into ten different locations), or "superstar" (checking into fifty different locations), while others are brand-specific, like the Top Chef Badge ("You wear the term 'foodie' as a badge of honor, and now have BRAVO's Top Chef Badge to prove it"). For a full list of Foursquare badges, see http://www.4squarebadges.com/foursquare-badge-list/.

6. http://www.rsmindex.com/ (accessed October 20, 2011).

7. Inamo restaurant in the United Kingdom features menus projected onto table tops, where diners can order food and drinks, choose a theme to suit their mood, and browse information about the neighborhood, including ordering a taxi after their meal (http://www.inamo-restaurant.com/pc/). Inamo was among the exhibitors at the i.Menu Expo in New York in November 2011, "designed for restaurant owners looking for new solutions using the Tablet technology (Like the Apple iPad or Android Tablets), Tablet Accessories, Web-based Applications, Cloud Services, and Mobile Merchant Partners as their new menu system and business back-end office solution" (http://www.imenuexpo.com/iMenu_Expo/Welcome.html, accessed November 25, 2011).

8. http://www.lousytippers.com/ (accessed November 15, 2011).

9. Disindividuation does not always result in negative behavior, but rather a shift toward the crowd psychology, which in some circumstances could be more benevolent than the individual's choices (Reicher, Spears and Haslam 2010).

10. Bourdain was reportedly surprised at the photograph the Travel Channel chose to use of him for their HD advertising campaign. It features the chef in a pool of blue water—or in his words, "after a horrifying night of drinking in Iceland, huddled, near naked in the Blue Lagoon, pondering whether to throw up or simply sink beneath the surface and die" (quoted in Neal 2008). In November 2011, another picture of Bourdain skinny-dipping (or rather floating on a lilo in a swimming pool with a beer) also made the social media rounds after being "dug up" by TMZ, this one apparently taken by his ex-wife in 1999. In response, his current wife tweeted that he "look[s] like beef jerky in those pics," and that he is "one step closer to becoming a Kardashian" (quoted in Shelasky 2011).

11. See also DeBaise 2011, who reports on chefs finding Twitter to be a "time suck," but valuable for business nevertheless.

12. http://www.cooknscribble.com/(accessed November 5, 2011). O'Neill's online classes join the ranks of existing resources for food writers, notably Gary Allen's 1999 *Resource Guide for Food Writers* and Dianne Jacobs' 2005 *Will Write for Food*.

13. http://drivers.lexus.com/lexusdrivers/magazine/articles/Lexus-News/news_2011_08_25 (accessed November 10, 2011).

Conclusion

(How) Is the Internet Changing the Way You Think About Food?

In Plato's *Phaedrus*, written around 370 BCE, Socrates tells the story of the Egyptian god Theuth, whose "great discovery was the use of letters"—in other words, writing. In conversation with the god Thamus (also the "king of the whole country of Egypt"), Theuth proposes that writing will "make Egyptians wiser and give them better memories," to which Thamus counters that on the contrary,

> this discovery of yours will create forgetfulness in the learners' souls, because they will not use their memories. . . . The specific which you have discovered is an aid not to memory, but to reminiscence, and you give your disciples not truth, but only the semblance of truth; they will be hearers of many things and will have learned nothing; they will appear to be omniscient and will generally know nothing; they will be tiresome company, having the show of wisdom without the reality. (Plato 2008)

Socrates uses Thamus's response to convey his own suspicion that writing would diminish the art of rhetoric: once words are committed to paper, they are "tumbled about anywhere among those who may or may not understand them," whereas the spoken and unwritten word can—in Socrates's reckoning—"defend itself, and knows when to speak and when to be silent."

This is just one early example of a long history of suspicion toward new technologies (presumably harbored by those Gopnik (2011) dubs the "Better-Nevers") and how they might negatively affect or replace the received, or "normal" way of doing things. In the eighteenth century the French statesman Malesherbes warned that newspapers could cause social isolation (it was then "normal" for people to get their news en masse from the pulpit); in the nineteenth century, schools were thought to ruin children's bodies by "protracted imprisonment"; in the twentieth, television threatened to kill conversation, and reading, and the radio (Bell 2010). In this century, one of the pressing anxieties is summarized by questions like, "How Is the Internet Changing the Way You Think?," as *Edge*'s World Question Center framed its annual "Big Question" in 2010 (Brockman 2010). The responses were as varied as the respondents, who included writers, actors, artists, and scientists like cognitive psychologist Steven Pinker, whose notable answer was, "Not At All." Pinker's response reflects one scientific perspective, which is that there is no—or not yet enough—evidence to support the idea that the Internet is messing with us on a neurological level. Or, as Harvard philosopher and neuroscientist Joshua Greene put it, "The Internet hasn't changed the way we think anymore [sic] than the microwave oven has changed the way we digest food" (quoted in Brockman 2010). Yet the fact of the question, and more specifically that it asks *how* the Internet affects us, rather than the more simple *does* the Internet affect us, presumes that changes are felt. Here, the science is less important than the experience (including conjectures about future experiences), and this is no less true when it comes to food and the Internet, where the merits of technological advances are routinely pitted against fears of what those same advances might do to the "normal" way of thinking about food.

Consider the question that Julia Moskin (2001b) put to *New York Times* readers in the run-up to Thanksgiving in 2011: Are cookbooks obsolete? Reporting on the phenomenal growth of the market for cooking apps designed for tablet computers (now typically with features such as infographics or animations, short instructional videos, voice guidance, hyperlinks, and timers), Moskin suggested that cookbooks "covered in splatters and sticky notes" will soon be things of the past, as will "recipes that exist only as strings of words." She is not unconvinced by the usefulness of the technology, which she describes as cognitively stimulating (and potentially useful for social networking):

> The interface of a tablet offers possibilities to the cook that would be impossible with a laptop, let alone a book. Swiping, tapping and zooming through information presented in multimedia is a good match for the experience of cooking, which involves all the senses of the brain, as well. And when those faculties fail, as often happens in high-stress kitchen scenarios like Thanksgiving, apps can come to the rescue with features like technique videos, embedded glossaries and social media links. (Moskin 2011b)

But her titular question does evoke a sadness at the possibility of an affirmative answer, particularly as she later describes cookbooks as having "long offered their own kind of enriched content, in the form of scribbles left in the margins by cooks who found they liked a little extra cinnamon, or a higher oven temperature." Indeed her question is not an empirical question at all, but rather a speculation at the possibility of a future without cookbooks.

The main impression here—and one that is also supported by Moskin's earlier dissatisfaction with recipe search engines, preferring the site that sent her back to her own bookshelf (Moskin 2011a)—is that cookbooks carry some weight of history. They may in the end be less useful or less user-friendly than apps, but they are "enriched" by traces of their past users (and also, we might add, by narratives that make the best cookbooks as good to read as they are to cook from).[1] Apps, however, are enriched for their users but retain no visible reminders of their use in the kitchen and are therefore less personal. (David Leite [2010] incidentally considers the fact of "no more pages stuck together with crusty egg whites" to be a particular advantage of using an iPad in the kitchen, while Michael Pollan is a fan of Mark Bittman's app but wishes someone would invent a "cook-proof iPad with some sort of kitchen condom," quoted in Thelin 2011.)

The other notion is the one that animates most historical anxieties about new technology, namely obsolescence, or the idea that the innovation will replace what came before it. Sometimes this is indeed the case, and with good reason: DVDs are an infinitely better product than video cassettes, and Blu-Ray discs further optimize the viewing experience (until someone invents something better). But as food writer Melissa Altman pointed out in her response to Moskin's article, her standard answer to the inevitable question of, "When, exactly, do you think the digital world will kill cookbooks?" she gets asked at conferences is, "Never":

> Publishing is a sometimes fearful, ancient business that has, for the last ten years, been chewing on its collective fingers over what I call monomedia, or the belief that readers will get their information one way and one way only, exclusively, and not from books because they're not sexy enough to compete with digitalia. To be clear, there is no question that cooking apps have claimed a seat at the publishing table, and rightly so: the ability to watch and re-watch Dorie Greenspan feel and poke biscuit dough so that you can actually see its correct consistency is unmistakably brilliant and enormously valuable. . . . But to claim that the advent of the cooking app is going to render cookbooks obsolete is misguided; the digital must complement print, and vice versa . . . (Altman 2011)

Altman's point coincides with other media commentators who dismiss the idea of new media as replacement, arguing rather that new Web technologies like YouTube merely extend and complement existing media like television and cinema, and that the Internet is "entirely parasitic" on more traditional media like television, books, magazines, radio, and so on (West 2007). [2]

It is true that paper publishers—perhaps most notably newspapers—are impacted by the rise of digital publication (budget cuts in newsrooms naturally also threaten the jobs of journalists, and therefore potentially the quality of news content produced). It is also the case that in times of economic stress, apps or e-cookbooks (or iBooks, which sites like Cookstr offer) might be the more attractive option to consumers than expensive cookbooks. Yet it is also true that amid the frenzy of producing, buying, and trying cooking apps, "traditional" cookbooks continue to enjoy enormous popularity, particularly those by celebrity chefs, and even more so those by celebrity chefs who also have TV shows. These books are often heavily discounted thanks to the "guaranteed popularity of books based on television programmes," leading British retailers to expect that a cookbook authored by Jamie Oliver would be the overall best seller during Christmas 2011 (Malnick 2011). (In 2010, sales of Oliver's *30-Minute Meals* surpassed those of any nonfiction book sold in the UK ever.) Reporting on the situation in the United States in 2009 for the *Wall Street Journal*, Laura Miller (2009) similarly noted that sales of books in the "cooking/entertaining" category were 4 percent higher than the previous year, while general adult nonfiction had dropped 9 percent, and that the most popular cookbooks were by no means "penny-pinching titles" but included "costly and highly impractical cookbooks by adulated chefs like Thomas Keller and Grant Achatz."

Occupying a rather different camp from Julia Moskin, Miller begins her article by declaring, "The cookbook ought to be dead. Like the compact disc, it uses an inconvenient and relatively expensive physical medium to deliver content that can be found, free, on the Web." Yet cookbooks have persisted so far and might very well continue to do so despite the potential inconvenience of price, size, impractical content, and crusty pages. Or it could be *because* of their potential inconveniences: cookbooks have always had an aspirational quality to them. This means that either they represent the things you wish you could make but never get a round to for a variety of reasons (catching your own hare is quite impractical, as is cooking Thomas Keller–style without an induction plate or sous-vide machine in your kitchen), or if you have the time and resources, you enjoy pushing the bounds of "normal" in the kitchen (you probably do catch your hare, slaughter it yourself, sous-vide it for several days, and then blog about it). So, the more apt conclusion to draw from the availability of multiple forms of food media is not that one or the other is under the threat of extinction—as the 2010 magazine campaign asked, did instant coffee kill coffee?—but rather that they simply provide more choice and also the ability, to use a media buzzword, to "customize" our experiences.[3]

Because we have available multiple ways of consuming information about food, we also have a multitude of ways of expressing how we think about food, and as Altman noted, the "monomedia" approach is increasingly rare. It often looks dichotomous—cookbooks vs. apps, YouTube vs. television, or "Foodies vs. Techies" as Virginia Hefferman sketches one distinction in the *New York Times*, where she dismisses James Beard and Julia Child in favor of Poppy Cannon, early enthusiast of convenience foods and "much-mocked author of *The Can-Opener Cookbook*" :

> If Cannon were around today, she'd be breaking WiFi passwords, turning her iPhone into a hotspot and otherwise pulling off better-mousetrap feats that would confound her traditionalist peers, just as her brisk celebration of America as "the land of the mix, the jar, the frozen-food package" infuriated Beard and company, who saw America instead as a land of coastal summer homes and hors d'oeuvres. . . . Let the foodies complain about Twitter while they make emu-egg cassoulet with crème fraiche. Techies have better things to do. (Hefferman 2011)

While she is certainly correct in highlighting that different people have different priorities, Hefferman's distinction does not survive her (otherwise funny) conclusion. "Foodies" might well distinguish themselves by choosing labor over efficiency when it comes to food—or "real" over "convenient" food—but that does not mean eschewing technology. (Who, these days, would make an emu-egg cassoulet and *not* tweet about it?) Part of the reason that we know as much as we do about food(ie)-culture, including cookbooks, is thanks to specific technologies like social media, and to the Internet in general, which in many cases serve to preserve the knowledge contained in "traditional" media. Blogger Carol Blymire has probably done more to immortalize the flagship cookbooks of both Thomas Keller and Grant Achatz than the chefs themselves by cooking her way through *The French Laundry Cookbook* and *Alinea* and blogging about the process.[4] Disciples of the *Larousse Gastronomique* (which is to say foodies, or historians, or both) can read about this iconic book's evolution from 1938 to its 2009 incarnation on The Gastronomer's Bookshelf, a blog dedicated to reviewing "all things food and wine" (Markham 2009). Now a century and a half old, the British classic *Mrs. Beeton's Book of Household Management* was recently remembered—and cooked from—in the pages of the *Economist*'s magazine, *This Intelligent Life*, available in print and online (Hirst 2011). All of which is not to forget the digital archives of historic cookbooks that are invaluable for food media scholarship.[5]

What is evident, then, is that thinking about food through digitized media has become mainstream, much like microwaves have become a standard feature of modern kitchens. But like microwaves do not preclude people from cooking or change how we digest food, less evident is whether this kind of digitized experience represents a loss, and if it does, whether that loss is necessarily a bad thing. One distinction that is worth invoking here is the difference between form and content. Although digital media provide us with many more forms through which to think about, and to talk about, and thereby to experience food, they do not necessarily impact the content of what we choose to pay attention to. Think about a recipe for hummus. On Twitter it may be condensed into 140 characters. A mobile app may deliver it with an infographic and a handy shopping list. A cookbook or a blog post may include a personal story about how it evokes a childhood memory for the writer, or a historical explanation of how it fits into a traditional meze—sometimes written as mezze—spread, including which is the correct spelling for the latter. For the person looking to create this dish, these different forms of media can be equally functional, and who is to say that the least embellished form will not produce the tastiest results? These are each different forms for thinking about food, but the form need not affect what or how we think. What we might need, instead, is simply to get used to the idea of multiple formats co-existing, ideally complementing one another, and at best performing a service for history. When historian Amy Bentley first watched a video of a grandmother cooking on YouTube, she was excited because "such a phenomenon seems to be the next logical step to preserving traditions in general" (quoted in Lindeman 2010). And as Fran Brennan put it in an article on "The Joy of Cooking in a Digital World": "I still have—and treasure—handwritten recipes and notes from both my mom and grandmother; and I'll use them forever. But I suspect the legacy I leave my own daughter will be far different: a bookmark folder full of links to recipes for all manner of food from all corners of the world. I do miss that backyard fence, and I can't believe I'm saying this. But I'm really okay with that" (Brennan 2011).

Like conversations about the effects of the Internet on our brains and habits, ruminations about the consequences of digital technology on our food experiences will likely continue for as long as they are no longer novel, and therefore no longer registered as consequences. Although the consequences are still up for debate, including which of them—if any—warrant direct concern, it is worth cataloging some of the unique developments in thinking about food that would have been impossible without Internet and that may soon be taken for granted (if they are not already). Previous chapters in this book have already chronicled some of these phenomena, like community building through blogging about food, challenges to intellectual property rights in an age of sharing, the shifting landscape of restaurant criticism now that "everyone is a critic," and how social media platforms have become integral to both the business and the pleasure of food.

In addition to housing digital archives (not only of cookbooks, but also of food blogs, and food studies programs), the Internet has also become a vital resource for academic discussions about food. This is not only through e-mail listservs such as that hosted by the Association for the Study of Food and Society (ASFS), but also "webinars," or seminars that are conducted online.[6] Some of these may only hold appeal to specialized audiences, but it is in line with the so-called democratizing force of the Web that more and more of what used to only be available to exclusive audiences can now be accessed by anyone with an Internet connection, anywhere in the world. The Science & Cooking Public Lectures at Harvard University, featuring such superstar chefs as Ferran Adrià, David Chang, and Grant Achatz, are archived on YouTube (Adrìa used the occasion of his lecture to announce plans for his El Bulli Foundation as a "social networking site of culinary creativity"). When journalist Corby Kummer, scientist/cook/author Harold McGee, and Ferran Adrià met for a public conversation on the subject of "A Day at elBulli" at the New York Public Library in 2008, the event was filmed and remains available on the library's website.[7]

The Robert Smith Hotel in New York City, home to a series of events called "Edible Conversation" featuring "authors of recently published books on food and drinks that have changed America and the world," hosted its first Food Writers' Conference in 2010, videos of which are also available on-line.[8] In metanarrative fashion, the conference featured panels dedicated to subjects like "The Future of Food Writing on the Internet," "From Websites to Blogs to Facebook," and "TV and Beyond—Future of Food & Cooking in Broadcast Media." During the last panel, author and food scholar Krishnendu Ray addressed the question of television dying with the retort that "so are we," and moderator Kathleen Collins (author of *Watching What We Eat: The Evolution of Television Cooking Shows*) closed the session by thanking all the participants for such a rich discussion and "wishing that we could package this in a text . . . [to] take it home." Collins was right that it was a rich discussion but missed that the camera in the room meant that it was available to take home—both for the participants and, crucially, for those people (like this writer) who could not be there in person. Online TED talks, finally, provide proverbial food for thought in practically every discipline, including food.[9] Previous speakers have included food world luminaries like Michael Pollan, Mark Bittman, Dan Barber, Jamie Oliver, and most recently historian Ken Albala, who explained during his talk why he believes that cookbooks are partly responsible for how little people cook and suggested that we "lose" them in order to get back in the kitchen (Albala 2011).

These examples are not direct products of social media, but they are communicated through social media platforms like Twitter and Facebook. So too are charity initiatives driven through food-centric social networks. Following the 2011 earthquake and tsunami in Fukushima, Japan, one food blogger (as she tells it) asked herself, "'What would Lady Gaga do?' The answer revealed itself. Get naked" (Nicholson 2011). With the help of eighteen fellow bloggers, the result was the cookbook *Nudie Foodies: Food Bloggers Peel for Japan* (featuring recipes and blogger flesh), 100 percent of the proceeds of which went to relief efforts in Japan. Vancouver-based Bake for the Quake was another social media initiative aimed at raising funds for Doctors Without Borders working in Japan after the same earthquake. Bloggers Without Borders (BWoB) is not exclusively food-focused but was inspired by witnessing the massive outpouring of support from the food blogging community for fellow blogger Jennifer Perillo following the death of her husband. In addition to focusing their efforts on #afundforjennie, started by Perillo's friends, other BWoB initiatives include "Dine In Irene," by which people can support farmers impacted by Hurricane Irene by hosting a dinner or a potluck party. The Foodspotting Spotathon creates challenges for users to "spot" a particular foodstuff: "For each challenge completed by the Foodspotting community, the Foodspotting team will give a gift to a family in need through Heifer international." Prizes include sheep, a hive of honeybees, a flock of chicken, a pig, a garden, and a milk cow.[10]

The online community at BakeSpace provides a mentoring service that is not a charity venture per se but designed to connect "members who have specific culinary skills with those who are eager to learn."[11] This is one manifestation of the notion that social media can have a positive and tangible effect not only on how we think about food (in this case, on our possible inhibitions in the kitchen), but also on how we eat. More directly related to furthering "healthy" or "correct" eating, there are a growing number of mobile and tablet applications dedicated to improving eating habits. Fooducate scans barcodes, retrieves reviews of the product in question, and suggests alternatives if the chosen product is considered "unhealthy." As *Chow*'s coverage of the app explained it, "The goal is that Fooducate will not only educate consumers but will force the FDA and food producers to stop making American kids into chubby chemical receptacles" (Santopietro 2011). Mealsnap is one of several apps designed to help users keep track of calories consumed, but with the difference that this one estimates calories by first taking a photograph of your food (Mealsnap is produced by DailyBurn, which also offers a FoodScanner app for those who prefer to calculate calories based on barcodes). Also in the research pipeline is a study on the possible effectiveness of sending tailored text messages to teens as a weight-loss intervention (Stein 2011), and HealthxDesign, the initiative that would "smarten" supermarkets by providing "a tech-enable shopping cart that calculates the nutritional quality of its contents and spurs real-time competition among shoppers to select healthy food." Possible directions for HealthxDesign include the idea of a mobile game where shoppers' purchases feed their online avatars, so people can observe the effects of their choices on future, virtual versions of themselves (Rich 2011).

Whether these applications and initiatives will work where others have so far not succeeded (for instance posting calorie counts on restaurant menus in an effort to reduce overconsumption) remains to be seen, but there remains an undeniable enthusiasm at the possibility that they *could*.[12] To be sure, the field of apps is perhaps the place where Kevin Kelly's belief in the "plausibility of the impossible" (Kelly 2005) is the most plain to see. Some apps are clearly very useful and to some already indispensable, like navigation systems, translators, coffee shop locators, and those that help to find and identify kosher and halal foods. Many more are useful and brilliant primarily for being able to do something that you never thought you would be able to do with your phone, like identifying that song that you hear in the coffee shop (Shazam), picking out a perfectly ripe melon (Melon Meter), or keeping an eye on the internal temperature of your roast from anywhere in the house (iGrill).

Even if apps and other Web attractions do not directly change the way we eat, there is some evidence to suggest that the distractions of the Internet can influence the amount of food that we eat. Reporting for *Salon* on one study of the eating habits of Korean teenagers, Sara Breselor (2010) tells us that the heaviest Web users "tend to eat smaller meals." She goes on to sketch a possible correlation between the trend of restaurants serving smaller "tasters" and our newly fragmented attention spans:

> Much has been made of the idea that the Internet has ruined out ability to focus on large, sustained ideas, books and long articles, and perhaps a trend toward smaller servings reflects our anxiety about decision-making in an information-saturated world. Committing to a single choice is much more difficult when your consciousness is so crowded by possible options. Even in a restaurant, where there are a finite number of choices, the same anxiety kicks in. The pear and arugula salad looks great, but what if the roasted beets are better? Perhaps this is why they new "small plates" menus are full of "combo" options that let diners cover a lot more ground that they could with a single full-size serving. (Breselor 2010)[13]

Web marketing specialist Dan Zarella takes Breselor's argument one step further, suggesting that the more important—or at least more prevalent—trend in eating is the "blending of offline and online." This means that when it comes to talking about restaurants using social media platforms like Twitter or Yelp, the person with the most influence is "not necessarily going to be judging restaurants by their culinary merits, but they'll be judging restaurants based on a social experience" (quoted in Breselor 2010).

Zarella's comments may be focused on eating out, but on the evidence of the vibrancy of food-blogging communities, the emphasis on creating a social experience through a mixture of offline (cooking and eating) and online (blogging or tweeting about cooking and eating) pervades much of the food world. It pervades much of the nonfood world too. According to Jonah Peretti, founder of the site Buzzfeed, home of "the hottest, most social content on the web":

> We used to think of the world in sections like front-page news, the sports section, the business section, the entertainment section. But when you think about memes and a lot of web culture, things are not organized that way. They're organized by a sort of social logic. What kind of things do people like to do together? What kinds of things do people relate to? We organize by these emotional responses. So we don't have a sports section and an entertainment section: we have a LOL [laughing out loud!] section, a WTF [good heavens!] section, a geeky section and so on. (quoted in Leith 2011, insertions in the original)

It is probably this kind of social logic that has led to the publication of a cookbook like Zach Golden's *What The F*@# Should I Make For Dinner?*, subtitled *The Answers to Life's Everyday Question (in 50 Fx@#ing Recipes)*. Based on a blog of the same name (or rather, on a blog called What The Fuck Should I Make For Dinner, because Web users are evidently less offended by curse words), it works by giving the reader three options for every recipe it provides: either make the recipe, or choose between, for example, "I don't fucking like that," or "I don't fucking eat meat," after which you will be directed to another recipe. But not everyone is impressed with the humor. *Chow*'s review of the book proposes that the "draw of the book, like the website, is the thrill certain people get from seeing the word *fuck* juxtaposed with, well, anything. . . . If blogging, food-related and otherwise, has taught us anything, it's that gimmickry can be a lucrative business, but also a hollow one. . . . And while it's entirely possible that plenty of folks will find the *WTF* cookbook worth the $10.20 it's selling for on Amazon, its existence has left us asking, well, what the fuck's the point?" (Marx 2011).

That is a question we can probably ask of a fair amount of what is available for our attention these days: what is the point of the Tumblr site Yelping with Cormac that imagines what Yelp reviews penned by Cormac McCarthy would look like? Then again, asking the question probably misses the point, which is not functional, but experiential. There is little "point" to an episode of *The Simpsons* (S23, E5) in which Marge, Bart, and Lisa take up food blogging—they are The Three Mouthketeers—except as a reflection of what people like. The episode's featured food rap sums up this particular social logic well, with references to "beepin' boppin' bulgogi," cooking turkey sous-vide style in a garbage bag, and wanting to be "Frank" like critic Frank Bruni, and "Ruthless" like food writer Ruth Reichl, and rhyming radicchio with (Tom) Colicchio.

Executive Producer Matt Selman acknowledges that the rap is "extremely silly, and the name is intentionally silly: 'Blogging a Food Blog.'" But he also calls the show a "love letter to foodie culture" (quoted in Sytsma 2011). Like Ruth Bourdain, and the *WTF* cookbook, these playful swipes at foodie culture are as much paeans to its ubiquity as they are challenges to the meaning—or the "point"—of that culture. One blogger did take the *Simpsons* episode as a wake-up call of sorts, suggesting that bloggers should "sit up and take notice" and subject themselves to the "Who Cares?" test every time they post: "Ask yourself, 'Who is going to care about this post?' You should have a good answer before you hit 'Publish'" (Wilder 2011).

Although the call to try to make social media activities meaningful to others is a laudable one, it also misses the extent to which those activities are at least as much about being in a network as they are about providing content. This means that the *activity* of blogging, or tweeting, or Facebooking, or Yelping—which is to say inhabiting the space of social media—is as important as what comes out of being there. In the end, the point may not be about how or whether the Internet is affecting how we think about food, but rather about acknowledging how social media provide us with so many more virtual locations for thinking about food, and for expressing those thoughts. As one writer put it, "a social network is not a product; it's a *place*" (Manjoo 2011c, emphasis in the original). With food on the brain, and in near constant demand by our bellies, it is a place we #occupy with gusto.

NOTES

1. See also Arnold-Ratliff (2011) on the "impending extinction" of recipe index cards, which, with their "grease stains" and "thumbprints," exist as "fragments of our personal histories."

2. See also Coady (2011, 277) on the "putative contrast between the Internet and the conventional media [which] is really no contrast at all. After all, many people consume what are by any standards conventional news-sources, such as the BBC, CNN, or *The New York Times*, on the Internet. Indeed it *could* be argued that declining newspaper readership is not symptomatic of a decline in the influence of conventional media at all, but merely a sign that more and more people are accessing conventional news sources on the Internet. In this view, the conventional media is simply embracing a new technology, just as it one embraced radio and television" (emphasis in the original).

3. "Did instant coffee kill coffee?" and "We Surf the Internet. We Swim in Magazines" were two slogans used for the 2010 "Power of Print" campaign (jointly launched by Condé Nast, Hearst Magazines, Meredith Corporation, Time Inc., and Wenner Media), designed to "promote the vitality of magazines as a medium" (http://multivu.prnewswire.com/mnr/

magazines/42679/, accessed June 13, 2011). See also Fahr 2010 for a Q&A with Amanda Hesser, whose answer to the question of whether she thinks that "the blogosphere and interactive websites . . . are in some way functioning as community cookbooks did in the past?" is that she "wouldn't say that they have ever gone away."

4. See French Laundry At Home (http://carolcookskeller.blogspot.com/, accessed September 17, 2011) and Alinea At Home (http://alineaathome.typepad.com/alinea_at_home/, accessed September 17, 2011).

5. See, for example, the archive of historic cookbooks at The Old Foodie (http://www.theoldfoodie.com/2006/12/online-historic-cookbooks.html, accessed August 1, 2011), and at Feeding America: The Historic American Cookbook Project (http://digital.lib.msu.edu/projects/cookbooks/, accessed October 13, 2011).

6. See, for example, Food Seminars International, which hosts regular webinars (http://www.foodseminarsinternational.com/webinars, accessed October 5, 2011), and once-off events like The Rock Ethics Institute at Penn State University, which in November 2011 hosted a Web presentation featuring Caroline Smith DeWaal, director of the Food Safety Program at the Center for Science in the Public Interest (http://rockethics.psu.edu/bios/dewaal.shtml, accessed November 20, 2011).

7. http://www.nypl.org/audiovideo/day-elbulli-ferran-adria-conversation-corby-kummer-harold-mcgee (accessed December 15, 2010).

8. http://rogersmithlife.com/the-art-of-food-2/roger-smith-food-writers-conference (accessed June 11, 2011).

9. An acronym for Technology, Entertainment, Design, TED is a nonprofit organization dedicated to "Ideas Worth Spreading." It holds an annual conference in Long Beach, California, and a number of satellite "TEDx" events around the world. There is also an annual TED prize of $100,000, which (as noted in chapter 3) for the first time it was awarded to a chef, went to Jamie Oliver in 2010 for his involvement in trying to improve school nutrition.

10. http://www.foodspotting.com/spotathon (accessed October 15, 2011).

11. http://www.bakespace.com/members/mentors/(accessed August 29, 2011).

12. On the inefficacy of calorie postings thus far, see Park 2011 and Elbel, Gyamfi, and Kersh 2011. On the possibilities and failings of health-focused apps, see Deck 2011.

13. See also Horovitz 2011, who reports that 35 percent of all food eaten by "Millenials" is snacks rather than "square" meals, and concludes that, "It's as if our social media habits are going right to our stomachs."

Bibliography

@twitter. 2011a. "#numbers." *Twitter blog*, March 14. Accessed August 6, 2011. http://blog. twitter.com/2011/03/numbers.html.

———. 2011b. "#YearInReview: Tweets Per Second." Twitter blog, December 6. Accessed December 7, 2011. http://blog.twitter.com/2011/12/yearinreview-tweets-per-second.html.

Albala, Ken. 2011. "Why We Don't Cook Anymore." *TEDxSanJoaquin*, November 2011. Accessed November 19, 2011. http://www.youtube.com/watch?v=rt-oaLVjz3U.

Altman, Melissa. 2011. "Reading, Apps, and the Myth of Cookbook Obsolescence." *Poor Man's Feast*, November 10. Accessed November 12, 2010. http://www.poormansfeast.com/ archives/reading-apps-and-the-myth-of-cookbook-obsolesence.html/.

Andriani, Lynn. 2009. "Judith Jones and Nora Ephron Talk About the Book's Power to Influence Young Cooks." *Publisher's Weekly*, July 20. Accessed March 14, 2011. http://web. archive.org/web/20091007215305/http://www.publishersweekly.com/article/CA6671678. html.

Angelo, Megan. 2011. "Time For Some Damage Control, Food Network: Ina Garten Just Snubbed A Make-A-Wish Kid." *Business Insider*, March 25. http://www.businessinsider. com/food-network-ina-garten-barefoot-contessa-make-wish-2011-3#ixzz1cvQrRQ2w

Antonoff, Michael. 2011. "Complaint Box: Pass the Flash, Please." *New York Times*, September 12. Accessed September 15, 2011. http://cityroom.blogs.nytimes.com/2011/09/12/ complaint-box-pass-the-flash-please/?hp.

Arnold-Ratliff, Katie. 2011. "The Rise and Fall of the Recipe Card." *Slate*, December 12, 2011, Accessed December 12, 2011. http://www.slate.com/articles/double_x/doublex/2011/12/ recipe_cards_a_brief_history.html.

Aronica, Molly. 2010. "Shop Like a Chef, With the Help of Your Favorite Food Celebrities." Daily Meal, April 14. Accessed December 2, 2010. http://www.thedailymeal.com/shop-chef-help-your-favorite-food-celebrities#ixzz1dI5o2rE0.

———. 2011. "More People Read User Reviews Than Restaurant Critics." *Daily Meal*, August 23. Accessed August 30, 2011. http://www.thedailymeal.com/where-do-you-get-your-restaurant-recommendations#ixzz1ax12zpD7.

Barbour, Celia. 2007. "For Orange Zest, Substitute Kool-Aid." *New York Times*, March 21, . Accessed March 22, 2007. http://www.nytimes.com/2007/03/21/dining/21twea.html.

Beale, Victoria. 2011. "Ground-Blog Day Julie and Julia Marathon Grinds on–and Stands Up." *The Guardian*, February 4. Accessed February 15, 2011. http://www.guardian.co.uk/film/ filmblog/2011/feb/04/blog-julie-julia-marathon-day-year.

Belasco, Warren. 2006. *Meals to Come: A History of the Future of Food*. Berkeley: University of California Press.

Bell, Vaughan. 2010. "Don't Touch That Dial!: A History of Media Technology Scares, from the Printing Press to Facebook." *Slate*, February 15, Accessed February 27, 2010. http://www.slate.com/articles/health_and_science/science/2010/02/dont_touch_that_dial.html.

Benn, Evan S. 2010. "Restaurant Reviewing Reaches Warped Speed." *STLToday*, November 6. http://www.stltoday.com/entertainment/dining/restaurants/article_23d1fdc4-5a75-5358-a159-99c94b1b0b3c.html.

Bennett, Sue, Maton, Karl, and Kervin, Lisa. 2008. "The 'digital natives' debate: A critical review of the evidence." *British Journal of Educational Technology* 39(5): 774–86.

Bercovici, Jeff. 2011. "Celebrity Chef Mario Batali Says Bankers As Bad As Hitler, Stalin." *Forbes*, November 8. Accessed November 10, 2011. http://www.forbes.com/sites/jeffbercovici/2011/11/08/celebrity-chef-mario-batali-says-bankers-as-bad-as-hitler-stalin/.

Berners-Lee, Tim. 2007. "Giant Global Graph." *Decentralized Information Group* (DIG), MIT, November 21. Accessed May 11, 2011. http://dig.csail.mit.edu/breadcrumbs/node/215.

Birdsall, John. 2011a. "Is Zagat Too Conservative for Google's Image?" *Chow*, September 8. Accessed October 1, 2011. http://www.chow.com/food-news/90458/is-zagat-too-conservative-for-google-s-image/.

———. 2011b. "The 2011 CHOW 13, Eddie Huang: Chefs Using Social Media." *Chow*, November 3. Accessed November 6, 2011. http://www.chow.com/food-news/95112/the-2011-chow-13/2/#wp_content.

BlogHer Food. 2011. "Recipe Writing: Copyright, Credit and Etiquette." BlogHer, Atlanta, May 21. Accessed June 3, 2011. http://www.blogher.com/liveblog-recipe-writing-copyright-credit-and-etiquette?wrap=node/364836/virtual-conference/posts.

Bloor, Duncan. 2011. "The Wheel of Hunger." *Search Insights*, September 28. Accessed October 29, 2011. http://searchinsights.wordpress.com/2011/09/28/the-wheel-of-hunger/.

Blymire, Carol. 2008. "Thank you." French Laundry At Home, October 23. Accessed May 17, 2011. http://carolcookskeller.blogspot.com/2008/10/thank-you.html.

Borrelli, Christopher. 2010. "Foodie Fatigue." *Chicago Tribune*, December 27. Accessed January 10, 2011. http://articles.chicagotribune.com/2010-12-27/features/ct-live-1227-foodie-backlash-20101227_1_foodies-breakfasts-plate.

Borzekowski, Dina L. G., Schenk, Summer, Wilson, Jenny L., and Peebles, Rebecka. 2010. "E-Ana and E-Mia: A Content Analysis of Pro–Eating Disorder Web Sites." *American Journal of Public Health* 100(8): 1526–34.

Brassfield, Marissa. 2011. "Twitter Thinspiration: The Kenneth Tong Twitter Campaign for Size-Zero Pills Fuels a Body-Image Frenzy." *CalorieLab*, January 9. Accessed January 17, 2011. http://calorielab.com/news/2011/01/09/twitter-thinspiration-the-kenneth-tong-twitter-campaign-for-size-zero-pills/.

Brennan, Fran. 2011. "Tweet Me Right: The Joy of Cooking in a Digital World." *Food52*, September 19. Accessed October 1, 2011. http://www.food52.com/blog/2522_tweet_me_right_the_joy_of_cooking_in_a_digital_world.

Breselor, Sara. 2010. "How the Web Is Changing the Way We Eat." Salon, May 10. Accessed May 11, 2010. http://www.salon.com/food/feature/2010/05/10/internet_changing_eating/index.html.

Brillat-Savarin, Jean-Anthelme. 1970. *The Philosopher in the Kitchen* [1825]. Harmondsworth: Penguin.

Brion, Raphael. 2010. "Denver Chef Calls Yelpers Inbred, Bored, Jobless Layabouts." *Eater*, November 10. Accessed March 13, 2011. http://m.eater.com/archives/2010/11/10/denver-chef-calls-yelpers-inbred-bored-jobless-layabouts.php.

———. 2011. "Alton Brown Leaves Twitter to 'Sick, Low Life Scumbags.'" *Eater*, August 4. Accessed August 29, 2011. http://eater.com/archives/2011/08/04/alton-brown-deletes-twitter-account.php.

Brockman, John. 2010. "A Big Question: 'How is the Internet Changing the Way you Think?'" *Edge*, June. http://edge.org/q2010/q10_print.html#responses.

Brooks, Zach. 2008. "On Banning Photography from Restaurants." Serious Eats, June 19, Accessed December 10, 2010. http://newyork.seriouseats.com/2008/06/banning-food-bloggers-photography-restaurants-momofuku-ko.html.

Brown, Alton. 2011a. "The Unfortunate Twitter Incident." *Alton Brown (just a lowly cook)*, August 4. Accessed October 10, 2011. http://altonbrown.com/2011/08/the-unfortunate-twitter-incident/.

———. 2011b. "Waffle, Anyone?"*Alton Brown (just a lowly cook)*, August 31. Accessed October 10, 2011. http://altonbrown.com/2011/08/waffle-anyone/.

———. 2011c. "My Fanifesto." *Alton Brown (just a lowly cook)*, September 19. Accessed October 10, 2011. http://altonbrown.com/2011/09/my-fanifesto/.

Bruni, Frank. 2007a. "For a Bad Boy Chef, He's Certainly Polite." *New York Times*, January 31. Accessed February 1, 2007. http://events.nytimes.com/2007/01/31/dining/reviews/31rest.html.

———. 2007b. "Giving Luxury the Thrill of Danger." *New York Times*, February 7. Accessed February 26, 2007. http://events.nytimes.com/2007/02/07/dining/reviews/07rest.html.

Buccafusco, Christopher J. 2007. "On the Legal Consequences of Sauces: Should Thomas Keller's Recipes be Per Se Copyrightable?" *Cardozo Arts & Entertainment Law Journal* 24: 1121–56.

Buford, Bill. 2006. *Heat: An Amateur's Adventure as Kitchen Slave, Line Cook, Pasta Maker and Apprentice to a Butcher in Tuscany*. London: Jonathan Cape.

Burkeman, Oliver. 2011. "SXSW 2011: The Internet Is Over." *The Guardian*, March 15. http://www.guardian.co.uk/technology/2011/mar/15/sxsw-2011-internet-online.

Burton, Brooke, and Greenstein, Leah. 2009. "Reviewers' Guidelines." Food Blog Code of Ethics, http://foodethics.wordpress.com/reviewers-guidelines/.

Carr, Nicholas. 2010a. "Tracking Is an Assault on Liberty, With Real Dangers." *Wall Street Journal*, August 6. Accessed August 15, 2010. http://online.wsj.com/article/SB10001424052748703748904575411682714389888.html.

———. 2010b. *The Shallows: What the Internet Is Doing to Our Brains*. New York: W.W. Norton & Company.

Champion, Ed. 2010. "The Cooks Source Scandal: How a Magazine Profits on Theft." *Reluctant Habits*, November 4. Accessed January 10, 2011. http://www.edrants.com/the-cooks-source-scandal-how-a-magazine-profits-on-theft/.

———. 2011. "Jason Allardyce: How a Sunday Times Journalist Ripped Off Ian Rankin, Bat Segundo, the Observer, and an Australian Producer." *Reluctant Habits*, April 24. Accessed August 10, 2011. http://www.edrants.com/jason-allardyce-how-a-sunday-times-journalist-ripped-off-ian-rankin-bat-segundo-the-observer-and-an-australian-producer/.

Chan, Suzanne. 2011. "When the Food Turned Sour . . ." Mom Confessionals, August 26. Accessed September 10, 2011. http://momconfessionals.com/2011/08/when-the-food-turned-sour/.

Chodorow, Jeffrey. 2007. "Letter to the Editor." *New York Times*, February 21. Accessed October 1, 2011. http://web.archive.org/web/20070223043501/http://www.chinagrillmgt.com/pdf/Response_NYTimes.pdf.

Chou, Jessica. 2011. "Worst Customer Ever: No Tip, Rude Message." Daily Meal, October 10. Accessed October 25, 2011. http://www.thedailymeal.com/worst-customer-ever-no-tip-rude-message.

Coady, David. 2011. "An Epistemic Defence of the Blogosphere." *Journal of Applied Philosophy* 28(3): 277–94.

Colaizzi, Merritt. 2010. "State of Social Media for Restaurants." *SmartBlog on Restaurants*, June 16. Accessed October 15, 2010. http://smartblogs.com/restaurants/2010/06/16/state-of-social-media-for-restaurants/.

Collins, Kathleen. 2009. *Watching What We Eat: The Evolution of Television Cooking Shows*. New York: Continuum.

Copyright. 2006. "Recipes." United States Copyright Office. Accessed June 20, 2007. http://www.copyright.gov/fls/fl122.html.

Cowen, Tyler. 2002. *Creative Destruction: How Globalization Is Changing the World's Cultures*. Princeton, NJ: Princeton University Press.

Crapanzano, Aleksandra. 2007. "Paris Match." *New York Times*, April 22. Accessed August 5, 2011. http://www.nytimes.com/2007/04/22/magazine/22food.t.html.

Dai, Lawrence. 2011a. "Day 80 – Reconciling the Two Julies." The Lawrence/Julie & Julia Project, February 17. Accessed February 20, 2011. http://lawrenceandjulieandjulia.blogspot.com/2011/02/day-80-reconciling-two-julies.html.

———. 2011b. "The Food in Julie & Julia vs. The Food I Eat (pt. 2)." The Lawrence/Julie & Julia Project, August 29. Accessed August 30, 2011. http://www.lawrenceandjulieandjulia.com/2011/08/day-273-food-in-julie-julia-vs-food-i.html.

———. 2011c. "Day 365 – The End." The Lawrence/Julie & Julia Project, November 29. Accessed November 30, 2011. http://www.lawrenceandjulieandjulia.com/2011/11/day-365-end.html.

Dalrymple, Theodore. 2010. "Thank You for Not Expressing Yourself." *New English Review*, March. Accessed March 7, 2010. http://www.newenglishreview.org/custpage.cfm/frm/58706/sec_id/58706.

Dean, Sam. 2011. "New Chef's Feed iPhone App Lets the Pros Do the Yelping." *Bon Appetit*, September 29. Accessed October 2, 2011. http://www.bonappetit.com/blogsandforums/blogs/badaily/2011/09/the-chefs-feed-app-lets-the-pr.html.

DeBaise, Colleen. 2011. "Foodies: Twitter a 'Time Suck' But Valuable." *Washington Post*, July 14. Accessed July 30, 2011. http://blogs.wsj.com/in-charge/2011/07/14/foodies-twitter-a-%E2%80%9Ctime-suck%E2%80%9D-but-valuable/.

Deck, Penny. 2011. "Yes, There's an App for That, But Does It Work?" *Feedback Solutions for Obesity*, May 19. Accessed June 30, 2011. http://feedbacksolutions.wordpress.com/2011/05/19/yes-theres-an-app-for-that-but-does-it-work/.

de Waal, Mandy. 2010. "Is your social network making you stupid?" Memeburn, September 17. Accessed October 15, 2010.http://memeburn.com/2010/09/is-your-social-network-making-you-stupid/.

Dias, Karen. 2003. "The Ana Sanctuary: Women's Pro-Anorexia Narratives in Cyberspace." *Journal of International Women's Studies* 4(2): 31–45.

DiCarlo, Louise. 2010. "Restaurants Are Eating up Social Media." *Three Village Patch*, October 13. Accessed January 15, 2011. http://threevillage.patch.com/articles/restaurants-are-eating-up-social-media.

Dignan, Larry. 2011. "Google Acquires Zagat, Enters Original Content Business." *ZDNet*, September 8. Accessed October 1, 2011. http://www.zdnet.com/blog/btl/google-acquires-zagat-enters-original-content-business/57611.

Dizik, Alina. 2011. "@Foodies: Peek into My Kitchen." *Wall Street Journal*, October 26. Accessed October 31, 2011. http://online.wsj.com/article/SB10001424052970204644504576653044135139376.html.

Dornenburg, Andrew, and Page, Karen. 1998. *Dining Out: Secrets from America's Leading Critics, Chefs, and Restaurateurs*. New York: John Wiley and Sons.

Downes, Lawrence. 2009. "Take 1 Recipe, Mince, Reduce, Serve." *New York Times*, April 21. Accessed January 15, 2011. http://www.nytimes.com/2009/04/22/dining/22twit.html.

du Lac, J. Freedom. 2011. "Solo Diners Find a New Companion Right at Their Fingertips." *Washington Post*, October 28. Accessed November 4, 2011. http://www.washingtonpost.com/local/solo-diners-find-a-new-companion-right-at-their-fingertips/2011/10/19/gIQAFPrCPM_story.html.

Dunlop, Rachael. 2011. "9 Vaccination Myths Busted. With Science!" Mamamia, October 4. Accessed October 4, 2011. http://www.mamamia.com.au/news/vaccination-myths-busted-by-science-cheat-sheet-on-immunisation/.

Dyson, Esther. 2011. "Attention Must Be Paid: How the Internet Is Changing How People Listen." *Slate*, September 20. Accessed October 1, 2011. http://www.slate.com/articles/business/project_syndicate/2011/09/attention_must_be_paid.html.

Edelstein, Ken. 2008. "AJC's Meridith Ford Goldman flouts a conflict of interest." *Creative Loafing Atlanta*, October 8. Accessed February 13, 2011. http://clatl.com/omnivore/archives/2008/10/08/ajcs-meridith-ford-goldman-flouts-a-conflict-of-interest/.

eGullet. 2006a. "Sincerest Form." *eGullet*, March 20. Accessed September 13, 2008. http://forums.egullet.org/index.php?/topic/84800-sincerest-form/.

———. 2006b. "The Merit of Preservation, Further Tales of Culinary Plagiarism." *eGullet*, June 20. Accessed September 13. http://forums.egullet.org/index.php?/topic/85783-the-merit-of-preservation/.

Elbel, Brian, Gyamfi, Joyce, and Kersh, Rogan. 2011. "Child and Adolescent Fast-Food Choice and the Influence of Calorie Labeling: A Natural Experiment." *International Journal of Obesity* 35(4): 493–500.

Fahr, Yasmin. 2010. "Q&A with Amanda Hesser of the *New York Times*." *Daily Meal*, November 8. Accessed December 5, 2010. http://www.thedailymeal.com/qa-amanda-hesser-new-york-times.

———. 2011. "Web Video Recipes: The Best and the Bizarre." *Daily Meal*, January 25. Accessed January 26, 2011. http://www.thedailymeal.com/web-video-recipes-best-and-bizarre.

Fallik, Dawn. 2011. "Ruth Reichl, James Beard Award Winners Cook up the Future of Food Writing." Poynter, May 25. Accessed May 25, 2011. http://www.poynter.org/latest-news/top-stories/133617/ruth-reichl-james-beard-award-winners-set-the-table-for-the-future-of-food-writing/.

Fauchart, Emmanuelle, and von Hippel, Eric. 2008. "Norms-based intellectual property systems: the case of French chefs." *Organization Science* 19(2): 187–201.

Fenster, Mike. 2011. "Obesity by the Numbers: Our Complex Relationship With Eating." *Atlantic*, September 28. Accessed September 30, 2011. http://www.theatlantic.com/life/archive/2011/09/obesity-by-the-numbers-our-complex-relationship-with-eating/245783/.

Forbes, Paula. 2011a. "Yelp Scolds Elite Yelpers for Degenerate Feeding Frenzies." *Eater*, March 22. Accessed October 1, 2011. http://eater.com/archives/2011/03/22/yelp-scolds-elite-yelpers-for-degenerate-feeding-frenzies.php.

———. 2011b. "Mario Batali Compares Bankers to Stalin, Hitler." *Eater*, November 9. Accessed November 10, 2011. http://eater.com/archives/2011/11/09/mario-batali-compares-bankers-to-stalin-hitler.php#more.

Ford Goldman, Meridith. 2008. "Feast fit for a bride." *Atlanta Journal-Constitution*, September 25. Accessed February 13, 2011. http://www.accessatlanta.com/restaurants/content/restaurants/stories/2008/09/25/meridith_ford_dishing.html.

Fortini, Amanda. 2011. "O Pioneer Woman!: The creation of a domestic idyll." *New Yorker*, May 9. Accessed May 25, 2011. http://www.newyorker.com/reporting/2011/05/09/110509fa_fact_fortini#ixzz1NNGehI7y.

Fox, Nick, Ward, Katie, and O'Rourke, Alan. 2005. "Pro-Anorexia, Weight-Loss Drugs and the Internet: An 'Anti-Recovery' Explanatory Model of Anorexia." *Sociology of Health and Illness* 27(7): 944–71.

Frank, Robert. 2011. "Food Fight: Top Chef's Roast of Bankers Lands Him in Hot Water." *Wall Street Journal*, November 10. Accessed November 10, 2011. http://online.wsj.com/article/SB10001424052970204358004577028552135309864.html.

Freeman, Danyelle. 2008. "Review Policy." Restaurant Girl. Accessed July 30, 2011. http://www.restaurantgirl.com/aboutus.html.

Gabler, Neal. 2011a. "Everyone's a Critic Now." *The Observer*, January 30. Accessed February 15, 2011. http://www.guardian.co.uk/culture/2011/jan/30/critics-franzen-freedom-social-network.

———. 2011b. "The Elusive Big Idea." *New York Times*, August 13. Accessed September 6, 2011. http://www.nytimes.com/2011/08/14/opinion/sunday/the-elusive-big-idea.html.

Gaudio, Monica. 2010. "Copyright Infringement and Me." *Illadore's House o Crack*, November 3. Accessed January 10, 2011. http://illadore.livejournal.com/30674.html.

Geitgey, Adam. 2002. "The Kaycee Nicole (Swenson) FAQ." In *We've Got Blog*, edited by John Rodzvilla, 89–98. Cambridge: Perseus.

Giordano, Dom. 2011. "The Barefoot Contessa Ina Garten's Recipe: Chilly Disdain for Leukemia patient Enzo Pereda." *Philadelphia Inquirer*, April 5. Accessed August 30, 2011. http://articles.philly.com/2011-04-05/news/29384780_1_ina-garten-contessa-sick-boy.

Gladwell, Malcolm. 2010. "Small Change: Why the Revolution Will Not Be Tweeted." *New Yorker*, October 4. Accessed November 20, 2010. http://www.newyorker.com/reporting/2010/10/04/101004fa_fact_gladwell.

Gold, Amanda. 2006. "Spain's Culinary Picasso Seeks New Inspiration." *San Francisco Chronicle*, November 8. Accessed March 20, 2007.http://www.sfgate.com/cgi-bin/article.cgi?file=/c/a/2006/11/08/FDGADM3JHL1.DTL.

Gold, Jonathan. 2010. "Two Cheers for Anonymity." *L.A. Weekly*, December 30. Accessed January 12, 2011. http://www.laweekly.com/2010-12-30/eat-drink/two-cheers-for-anonymity/.

Goldmark, Alex. 2011. "Lessons From the End of the Free Starbucks Card Experiment." Good, August 17. Accessed August 20, 2011. http://www.good.is/post/lessons-from-the-end-of-the-free-for-all-starbucks-card-experiment/.

Gopnik, Adam. 2011. "The Information: How the Internet Gets Inside Us." *New Yorker*, February 14. Accessed June 1, 2011. http://www.newyorker.com/arts/critics/atlarge/2011/02/14/110214crat_atlarge_gopnik.

Green, David Allen. 2011. "A Vile Tweet from the Disreputable @MrKennethTong." Jack of Kent, January 8. Accessed January 17, 2011.http://jackofkent.blogspot.com/2011/01/vile-tweet-from-disrepuatble.html.

Haas, Stephen M., Irr, Meghan E., Jennings, Nancy A., and Wagner, Lisa M.. 2011. "Communicating Thin: A Grounded Model of Online Negative Enabling Support Groups." *New Media & Society* 13(1): 40–57.

Hari, Johann. 2011a. "Promoting Anorexia: An Interview with Kenneth Tong. This Was No Hoax." *Huffington Post*, January 12. Accessed January 17, 2011. http://www.huffingtonpost.com/johann-hari/promoting-anorexia-an-int_b_807807.html.

———. 2011b. "A Personal Apology." *The Independent*, September 15. Accessed September 16, 2011. http://www.independent.co.uk/opinion/commentators/johann-hari/johann-hari-a-personal-apology-2354679.html.

Harper, Jim. 2010. "It's Modern Trade: Web Users Get as Much as They Give." *Wall Street Journal*, August 7. Accessed August 15, 2011. http://online.wsj.com/article/SB10001424052748703748904575411530096840958.html.

Harris, Sam. 2010. *The Moral Landscape: How Science Can Determine Human Values*. New York: Free Press.

Hastings, Chris, and Fisher, Deryn. 2012. "Twitter Crashes after 16,000 New Year Tweets a SECOND Lead to Meltdown." *The Daily Mail*, January 1. Accessed January 2, 2012. http://www.dailymail.co.uk/sciencetech/article-2080814/Twitter-outage-16k-Happy-New-Year-tweets-SECOND-lead-meltdown.html

Hayward, Tim. 2009. "Ethical Food Blogging." *The Observer*, May 6. Accessed May 11, 2011.http://www.guardian.co.uk/lifeandstyle/wordofmouth/2009/may/06/ethical-food-blog-code.

———. 2010. "How Right is the Customer Who Blogs?" *The Guardian*, November 5. Accessed November 6, 2010. http://www.guardian.co.uk/lifeandstyle/wordofmouth/2010/nov/05/food-and-drink1.

Hefferman, Virginia. 2011. "Foodies Vs. Techies." *New York Times*, May 15. Accessed May 16, 2011. http://opinionator.blogs.nytimes.com/2011/05/15/foodies-vs-techies/.

Hess, Amanda. 2011. "Google Plus Zagat Equals Yelp? Let's Hope Not." Good, September 8. Accessed October 1, 2011. http://www.good.is/post/google-and-zagat-we-don-t-need-another-yelp/.

Hesser, Amanda. 2011. "Google's New Recipe Search." Food52, March 24. Accessed March 25, 2011. http://www.food52.com/blog/1838_googles_new_recipe_search.

Hirsch, J. M. 2011. "Is It Bok Choy, Bok Choi, Pak Choy or Pak Choi?" J. M. Hirsch, May 16. Accessed May 22, 2011. http://www.jmhirsch.com/?p=1715.

Hirst, Christopher. 2011. "Through the Isinglass." *This Intelligent Life*, November/December. Accessed November 17, 2011. http://moreintelligentlife.com/content/lifestyle/christopher-hirst/through-isinglass.

Holahan, Catherine. 2007. "Yahoo's Feast for Foodies." *Business Week*, December 21. Accessed January 14, 2008. http://www.businessweek.com/technology/content/nov2006/tc20061103_962195.htm.

Horovitz, Bruce. 2011. "Marketers Adapt Menus to Eat-What-I-Want-When-I-Want Trend." *USAToday*, November 21. Accessed November 23, 2011. http://www.usatoday.com/money/industries/food/story/2011-11-21/weird-eating/51338542/1.

Howard, Rebecca Moore. 1995. "Plagiarisms, Authorships and the Academic Death Penalty." *College English* 57(7): 788–806.

Huffington Post. 2011a. "Boston Restaurant Turns Tables on Bad Reviews." *Huffington Post*, June 9. Accessed July 3, 2011. http://www.huffingtonpost.com/2011/06/09/boston-restaurant-funny-reviews_n_874396.html.

———. 2011b. "Allison Matsu Tweets About Bartender's Conversation At Houston's Own House Lounge, Gets Kicked Out." *Huffington Post*, August 18. Accessed August 25, 2011. http://www.huffingtonpost.com/2011/08/18/customer-tweets-gets-kicked-out_n_930253.html.

Hurst, Daniel. 2011. "Clever or Creepy? Restaurant's Web of Data." *The Sydney Morning Herald*, July 26. Accessed August 5, 2011. http://www.smh.com.au/entertainment/restaurants-and-bars/clever-or-creepy-restaurants-web-of-data-20110725-1hwfq.html.

Independent. 2011a. "New Foursquare 3.0 Rewards Diners Who Travel in Packs." *Independent*, March 11. Accessed March 20, 2011. http://www.independent.co.uk/life-style/food-and-drink/new-foursquare-30-rewards-diners-who-travel-in-packs-2238827.html.

———. 2011b. "Popular food channel gains more YouTube followers than Justin Bieber." *Independent*, July 25. Accessed July 29, 2011. http://www.independent.co.uk/life-style/food-and-drink/popular-food-channel-gains-more-youtube-followers-than-justin-bieber-2325892.html#.

Jacob, Dianne. 2010a. "Giving Recipes Away a Big Subject at IFBC." Will Write For Food, August 30. Accessed August 7, 2011. http://diannej.com/blog/2010/08/giving-recipes-away-a-big-subject-at-ifbc/.

———. 2010b. "Outrageous Blogger Request, and the Outcome." Will Write For Food, September 30. Accessed August 7, 2011. http://diannej.com/blog/2010/09/outrageous-blogger-request-and-the-outcome/.

———. 2011. "Smitten Kitchen's Deb Perelman on What She Learned by Writing a Cookbook." Will Write For Food, August 2. Accessed August 7, 2011. http://diannej.com/blog/2011/08/smitten-kitchens-deb-perelman-on-what-she-learned-by-writing-a-cookbook/.

Johnston, Josée, and Baumann, Shyon. 2010. *Foodies: Democracy and Distinction in the Gourmet Foodscape*. New York: Routledge.

Jones, Chris, and Czerniewicz, Laura. 2010. "Describing or Debunking? The Net Generation and Digital Natives." *Journal of Computer Assisted Learning* 26(5): 317–20.

Jones, Evan. 1990. *Epicurean Delight: The Life and Times of James Beard*. New York: Alfred A. Knopf.

Kahn, Joseph P. 2010. "Once You Hit Send, Privacy is Gone." *Boston Globe*, November 15. Accessed January 10, 2011. http://www.boston.com/ae/media/articles/2010/11/15/once_you_hit_send_you_can_forget_privacy/.

Kamp, David. 2006. *The United States of Arugula*. New York: Broadway Books.

Keen, Andrew. 2007. *The Cult of the Amateur: How Today's Internet is Killing Our Culture and Assaulting Our Economy*. London: Nicholas Brealey Publishing.

———. 2011. "Your Life Torn Open, essay 1: Sharing is a trap." *Wired*, February 3. Accessed February 19, 2011. http://www.wired.co.uk/magazine/archive/2011/03/features/sharing-is-a-trap.

Keet, Maggy. 2011. "A Fund For Jennie: The Final Update!" *Bloggers Without Borders*, October 17. Accessed November 15, 2011. http://www.bloggerswoborders.org/2011/10/a-fund-for-jennie-the-final-update/.

Kellog, Cecily. 2011. "Coping with Trolls, Griefers and Cyberbullies." MomCrunch, August 9. Accessed August 15, 2011. http://blogs.babble.com/momcrunch/2011/08/09/coping-with-trolls-griefers-and-cyberbullies/.

Kelly, Kevin. 2005. "We Are the Web." *Wired*, August 13. Accessed February 2, 2010. http://www.wired.com/wired/archive/13.08/tech.html.

Kessler, Jason. 2011. "I'm Sick of Food Trucks." *Bon Appétit*, May 10. Accessed June 13, 2011. http://www.bonappetit.com/blogsandforums/blogs/badaily/2011/05/im-sick-of-food-trucks.html.

Keyes, Jesse. 2011. "A Reviewer's Demise." *Huffington Post*, October 25. Accessed November 1, 2011. http://www.huffingtonpost.com/jesse-keyes/a-reviewers-demise_b_1031069.html.

Kinsley, Michael. 2011. "Requiem for a Governor before He's in the Ring." *Bloomberg*, September 30. Accessed October 1, 2011. http://www.bloomberg.com/news/2011-09-30/requiem-for-a-governor-before-he-s-in-the-ring-michael-kinsley.html.

Kinsman, Kat. 2011a. "McDonald's Offers Mom Bloggers a Seat at the Table." *Eatocracy*, July 27. Accessed August 5, 2011. http://eatocracy.cnn.com/2011/07/27/mcdonalds-offers-mom-bloggers-a-seat-at-the-table/.

———. 2011b. "Twitter, Feed Me." *Eatocracy*, October 5. Accessed October 10, 2011. http://eatocracy.cnn.com/2011/10/05/twitter-feed-me/.

Korsmeyer, Carolyn. 1999. *Making Sense of Taste: Food and Philosophy*. Ithaca, NY: Cornell University Press.

Ladybird. 2010. "Awkward Food Blogging Moments." Diary of a Ladybird, January 18. Accessed November 17, 2010.http://diaryofaladybird.blogspot.com/2010/01/awkward-food-blogging-moments.html.

Lam, Francis. 2010. "When Your Restaurant's Review Has Your Mom Crying." *Salon*, October 14. Accessed October 15, 2011. http://www.salon.com/food/francis_lam/2010/10/14/sam_sifton_eddie_huang.

Lanier, Jaron. 2010. *You Are Not a Gadget*. New York: Alfred A. Knopf.

Lasky, Ed. 2009. "Cass Sunstein's Despicable Ideas on Regulating the Internet." *American Thinker*, July 12. Accessed October 3, 2011. http://www.americanthinker.com/blog/2009/07/cass_sunsteins_despicable_idea.html.

Leite, David. 2010. "I Have Taken a Lover, the iPad." *Leite's Culinaria*, June 22. Accessed May 10, 2011. http://leitesculinaria.com/43860/writings-apple-ipad-cookbooks.html.

Leith, Sam. 2011. "You Are What You Meme: What Maru the Cat Says About Us." *Slate*, October 15. Accessed October 16, 2011. http://www.slate.com/articles/technology/ft/2011/10/what_memes_like_maru_the_cat_and_star_wars_kid_say_about_us.html.

Levenstein, Harvey. 2003. *Paradox of Plenty: A Social History of Eating in Modern America*. Berkeley: University of California Press.

Levine, Michael P., and Murnen, Sarah K. 2009. "Everyone Knows That Mass Media Are/Are Not [Pick One] a Cause of Eating Disorders: A Critical Review of Evidence for a Causal Link between Media, Negative Body Image, and Disordered Eating in Females." *Journal of Social and Clinical Psychology* 28(1): 9–42.

Liddle, Alan J. 2011. "Social Media Helps Spur Produce Consumption." *Restaurant News*, August 2. Accessed August 7, 2011. http://www.nrn.com/article/social-media-helps-spur-produce-consumption.

Lieber, Ron. 2010. "Zagat Survery Aims to Regains Its Online Balance." *New York Times*, November 13. Accessed November 20, 2010. http://www.nytimes.com/2010/11/14/technology/14zagat.html.

Lindeman, Scarlett. 2010. "YouTube: Better Than Cookbooks." *Atlantic*, December 8. Accessed January 11, 2011. http://www.theatlantic.com/food/archive/2010/12/youtube-better-than-cookbooks/67658/.

Lohr, Steven. 2010. "How Privacy Vanishes Online." *New York Times*, March 16. Accessed March 18, 2010. http://www.nytimes.com/2010/03/17/technology/17privacy.html.

Lynch, Rene. 2010. "Life is Good for Gluten-Free Girl." *Los Angeles Times*, November 11. Accessed November 20, 2011. http://www.latimes.com/features/food/la-fo-1104-gluten-free-girl-20101111,0,2827170.story.

———. 2011a. "Don't Forget to Take Your #weekendeats Pictures." *Los Angeles Times*, January 29. Accessed February 15, 2011. http://latimesblogs.latimes.com/dailydish/2011/01/dont-forget-to-take-your-weekendeats-pictures.html.

———. 2011b. "Barefoot Contessa Was Unaware of Request, but Will Now Host Her Young Fan." *Los Angeles Times*, March 28. Accessed August 15, 2011. http://latimesblogs.latimes. com/dailydish/2011/03/barefood-contessa-ina-garten-to-meet-host-one-of-her-youngest-fans.html.

———. 2011c. "Sarah Gim's Servings of Virtual Food Prove Irresistible." *Los Angeles Times*, March 31. Accessed April 5, 2011. http://www.latimes.com/features/food/la-fo-0331-sarah-gim-tastespotting-20110331,0,2601935.story.

Malnick, Edward. 2011. "Christmas 2011: Celebrity Chefs Battle Over Cookery Books." *The Telegraph*, November 6. Accessed November 10, 2011. http://www.telegraph.co.uk/ foodanddrink/foodanddrinkbooks/8871818/Christmas-2011-celebrity-chefs-battle-over-cookery-books.html.

Mama Pereda. 2011a. "March 2011 Update 2 – Make-A-Wish." *Angels for Enzo*. Accessed August 17, 2011. http://www.angelsforenzo.com/march2011update2.htm.

———. 2011b. "PLEASE STOP THE MADNESS." *Angels for Enzo*. Accessed November 2, 2011. http://www.angelsforenzo.com/pleasestopthemadness.htm.

Manjoo, Farhad. 2010. "This Is Not a Blog Post." *Slate*, October 15. Accessed October 16, 2010. http://www.slate.com/id/2271184/.

———. 2011a. "My PC Needs ESP." *Slate*, August 3. Accessed August 5, 2011.http://www. slate.com/id/2300808/.

———. 2011b. "Overdone: Why are restaurant websites so horrifically bad?" *Slate*, August 9. Accessed August 11, 2011. http://www.slate.com/articles/technology/technology/2011/08/ overdone.html.

———. 2011c. "Google+ Is Dead." *Slate*, November 8. Accessed November 9, 2011. http:// www.slate.com/articles/technology/technology/2011/11/google_had_a_chance_to_ compete_with_facebook_not_anymore_.html.

Mariani, John. 2009. "John Mariani, In His Own Words." Grub Street Chicago, May 18. Accessed October 1, 2011. http://chicago.grubstreet.com/2009/05/john_mariani_in_his_ own_words.html.

———. 2011. "What Your Favorite Restaurants Know About You." *Esquire*, November 8. Accessed November 10, 2011. http://www.esquire.com/blogs/food-for-men/great-restaurant-service-110811.

Marikar, Sheila. 2011. "'Barefoot Contessa's' Offer to Make-a-Wish Kid Backfires." *ABC News*, March 31. Accessed August 16, 2011. http://abcnews.go.com/Entertainment/ barefoot-contessas-offer-make-kid-backfires/story?id=13264867#.Tray3UNqZyg.

Markham, Duncan. 2009. "The Evolution of Larousse Gastronomique." *The Gastronomer's Bookshelf*, October 25. Accessed February 20, 2011. http://www.thegastronomersbookshelf. com/3664_the-evolution-of-larousse-gastronomique.

Martelle, Scott. 2005. "The Real Cost of a Free Meal." *Los Angeles Times*, November 2. Accessed October 1, 2011. http://articles.latimes.com/2005/nov/02/food/fo-mariani2.

Martin, Adam. 2011. "The End of the Career Food Critic." *Atlantic Wire*, September 14. Accessed September 20, 2011.http://www.theatlanticwire.com/national/2011/09/sam-sifton-departure-and-the-end-of-the-career-food-critic/42483/.

Marx, Rebecca Flint. 2011. "Foulmouthed Website Spawns Foulmouthed Book. WTF?" *Chow*, October 19. Accessed October 29, 2011. http://www.chow.com/food-news/94379/foul-mouthed-website-spawns-foul-mouthed-book-wtf/.

McLaughlin, Katy. 2006. "'That Melon Tenderloin Looks Awfully Familiar . . . '." *Wall Street Journal*, June 24. Accessed June 16, 2007. http://online.wsj.com/article/ SB115109369352989196.html.

McMahon, Barbara. 2007. "Review of Meal That 'Jangled Like a Car Crash' Deemed Defamatory." *The Guardian*, June 16. Accessed June 16, 2007. http://media.guardian.co.uk/site/ story/0,,2104346,00.html.

McWilliams, James. 2011. "McFib: The Awful Conditions at McDonald's McRib Pork Supplier." *Atlantic*, November 3. Accessed November 3, 2011. http://www.theatlantic.com/life/ archive/2011/11/mcfib-the-awful-conditions-at-mcdonalds-mcrib-pork-supplier/247779/.

Mennell, Stephen. 1985. *All Manners of Food: Eating and Taste in England and France from the Middle Ages to the Present*. Oxford: Basil Blackwell.

Meyrowitz, Joshua. 1985. *No Sense of Place: The Impact of Electronic Media on Social Behavior*. Oxford: Oxford University Press.

Miller, Laura. 2009. "A Recipe for Escapism." *Wall Street Journal*, May 2. Accessed February 10, 2011. http://online.wsj.com/article/SB124122464266979257.html.

Mitchell, John T. 2011. "Copyrighted Recipe for Scrambled Eggs." *CopyOwner: Competition, Copyright and Freedom of Expression*, May 29. Accessed August 22, 2011. http://interactionlaw.com/wordpress/2011/05/29/copyrighted-recipe-for-scrambled-eggs/.

Moskin, Julia. 2010. "When Is a Free Meal Just Part of a Writer's Job?" *New York Times*, June 29. Accessed August 5, 2010. http://www.nytimes.com/2010/06/30/dining/30comp.html.

———. 2011a. "Can Recipe Search Engines Make You a Better Cook?" *New York Times*, May 17. Accessed May 18, 2011. http://www.nytimes.com/2011/05/18/dining/can-recipe-search-engines-make-you-a-better-cook.html.

———. 2011b. "Are Cookbooks Obsolete?" *New York Times*, November 8. Accessed November 8, 2011. http://www.nytimes.com/2011/11/09/dining/are-apps-making-cookbooks-obsolete.html.

MrsCC. 2010. "Top Chef calls to rant about negative comments." *eGullet*, October 29. Accessed November 6, 2010. http://forums.egullet.org/index.php?/topic/135406-top-chef-calls-to-rant-about-negative-comments/.

Mulveen, Ruaidhri, and Hepworth, Julie. 2006. "An Interpretative Phenomenological Analysis of Participation in a Pro-Anorexia Internet Site and Its Relationship with Disordered Eating." *Journal of Health Psychology* 11(2): 283–96.

Murphy, Kate. 2010. "First Camera, Then Fork." *New York Times*, April 6. Accessed November 2, 2010. http://www.nytimes.com/2010/04/07/dining/07camera.html.

Myers, B. R. 2011. "The Moral Crusade against Foodies." *Atlantic*, March. Accessed February 9, 2011. http://www.theatlantic.com/magazine/print/1969/12/the-moral-crusade-against-foodies/8370.

Neal. 2008. "Adventures In Traumatic Advertising: Anthony Bourdain Edition." *Fishbowl NY*, February 28. Accessed November 1, 2011. http://www.mediabistro.com/fishbowlny/adventures-in-traumatic-advertising-anthony-bourdain-edition_b7936.

Newman, Andrew Adam. 2011. "Bloggers Don't Follow the Script, to ConAgra's Chagrin." *New York Times*, September 6. Accessed September 10, 2011.http://www.nytimes.com/2011/09/07/business/media/when-bloggers-dont-follow-the-script-to-conagras-chagrin.html.

Nichols, Martha. 2011. "Is There Too Much Food Writing?" *Athena's Head*, November 16. Accessed November 18, 2011. http://open.salon.com/blog/martha_nichols/2011/11/16/is_there_too_much_food_writing.

Nicholson, Linda Miller. 2011. "Nude for Good? Food Bloggers Peel for Japan." *Nudie Foodies*, April 9. Accessed September 30, 2011. http://thenudiefoodies.com/2011/peel-it-off-for-japan/.

Nielsen, Angela. 2011. "Still Think Social Media is A Fad?" *Inspired Mag*, April 28. Accessed June 30, 2011. http://www.inspiredm.com/social-media-fad/.

Norton, James. 2011a. "Are Yelpers Foochebags"? *Chow*, March 23. Accessed October 1, 2011. http://www.chow.com/food-news/76985/are-yelpers-foochebags/.

———. 2011b. "The High-Tech Smearing of Ina Garten." *Chow*, March 29. Accessed August 15, 2011. http://www.chow.com/food-news/77531/the-high-tech-smearing-of-ina-garten/.

O'Neill, Brendan. 2011. "The Reaction to Twitter's 'Anorexia Promoter' Kenneth Tong Was Mostly Hysterical Nonsense." *Telegraph*, January 13. Accessed January 17, 2011. http://blogs.telegraph.co.uk/news/brendanoneill2/100071844/the-reaction-to-twitters-anorexia-promoter-kenneth-tong-was-mostly-hysterical-nonsense/.

Orenstein, Peggy. 2010. "I Tweet, Therefore I Am." *New York Times Magazine*, July 30. Accessed August 15, 2010. http://www.nytimes.com/2010/08/01/magazine/01wwlnlede-t.html.

Ozersky, Josh. 2010. "Great Wedding Food: Tips from a Newly Married Critic." *Time*, June 15. Accessed August 5, 2010. http://www.time.com/time/nation/article/0,8599,1996593,00.html.

Pariser, Eli. 2011. "Beware Online 'Filter Bubbles'." *TED*, February. Accessed May 3, 2011. http://www.thefilterbubble.com/ted-talk.

Park, Alice. 2011. "Study: Calorie Counts in Restaurants May Not Curb Eating Habits." *Time*, 14 January. Accessed January 17, 2011. http://healthland.time.com/2011/01/14/study-calorie-counts-in-restaurants-may-not-curb-eating-habits/#ixzz1BGYJ3ofj.

Paul, Michael J., and Dredze, Mark. 2011. "You Are What You Tweet: Analyzing Twitter for Public Health." *Human Language Technology Center of Excellence, John Hopkins University*. Accessed September 29, 2011. http://www.cs.jhu.edu/~mpaul/files/2011.icwsm.twitter_health.pdf.

Pepitone, Julianne. 2011. "Your New Waiter Is a Tablet." *CNN*, May 16. Accessed June 30, 2011. http://money.cnn.com/2011/05/16/smallbusiness/e_la_carte/.

Perillo, Jennifer. 2011. "for mikey." *In Jennifer's Kitchen*, August 9. Accessed August 11, 2011. http://www.injennieskitchen.com/2011/08/for-mikey.html.

Phipps, Catherine. 2011. "From Blogs to Books." *The Guardian*, June 6. Accessed June 13, 2011. http://www.guardian.co.uk/lifeandstyle/wordofmouth/2011/jun/06/from-blogs-to-books.

Pierce, Tony. 2005. "The History of Blooks." Busblog, October 11. Accessed June 7, 2010. http://busblog.tonypierce.com/2005/10/history-of-blooks-by-tony-pierce.html.

Pingdom. 2010. "Internet 2010 in numbers." Pingdom, January12. Accessed March 15, 2011. http://royal.pingdom.com/2011/01/12/internet-2010-in-numbers/.

Plato. 2008. *Phaedrus* [370 BCE]. Project Gutenberg. Accessed November 5, 2010. http://www.gutenberg.org/files/1636/1636-h/1636-h.htm#2H_4_0002.

Pollack, Malla. 1991. "Intellectual Property Protection for the Creative Chef, or How to Copyright a Cake: A Modest Proposal." *Cardozo Law Review* 12(1477): 1–85.

Prensky, Mark. 2001. "Digital Natives, Digital Immigrants." *On the Horizon*, 9(5). Accessed February 2010. http://www.albertomattiacci.it/docs/did/Digital_Natives_Digital_Immigrants.pdf.

PWSux. 2011a. "Mike is No Longer Retarded . . . " The Pioneer Woman Sux, February 28. Accessed March 4, 2011. http://www.thepioneerwomansux.com/2011/02/mike-is-no-longer-retarded/.

———. 2011b. "Allow me to explain, Cecily." The Pioneer Woman Sux, August 11. Accessed August 15, 2011. http://www.thepioneerwomansux.com/2011/08/allow-me-to-explain-cecily/.

Qualman, Erik. 2009. Socialnomics: *How Social Media Transforms the Way We Live and Do Business*. Hoboken, NJ: John Wiley & Sons.

Quinn, Eugene R. 1999–2007. "The Law of Recipes." IP Watchdog, Inc. Accessed February 27, 2011. http://web.archive.org/web/20090227133000/http://www.ipwatchdog.com/copyright/the-law-of-recipes/.

Radford, Benjamin. 2007. "Media and Mental Health Myths: Deconstructing Barbie and Bridget Jones." *The Scientific Review of Mental Health Practice* 5(1): 81–87.

Rayner, Jay. 2006. "Meet Mr Bruni, the Man Who Can Spoil Gordon's NY Party." *The Observer*, November 12. Accessed November 15, 2006. http://www.guardian.co.uk/food/Story/0,,1945969,00.html.

Reicher, Stephen, Spears, Russell, and Haslam, S. Alexander. 2010. "The Social Identity Approach in Social Psychology." In *The SAGE HandBook of Identities*, edited by Margaret Wetherell and Chandra T. Mohanty, 45–62. London: Sage.

RestaurantNews. 2010. "New TextMyFood™ Service Tested Successfully At Boston Restaurants." Restaurant News, October 29. Accessed December 2, 2010. http://www.restaurantnews.com/new-textmyfood-service-tested-successfully-at-boston-restaurants/.

Rich, Sarah. 2011. "A Better Way to Fight Obesity: New, Smarter Supermarkets." *Atlantic*, May 12. Accessed May 13, 2011. http://www.theatlantic.com/life/archive/2011/05/a-better-way-to-fight-obesity-new-smarter-supermarkets/238813/.

Roberts, Adam. 2011. "How To Support Yourself As A Food Blogger." *Amateur Gourmet*, October 27. Accessed November 10, 2011. http://www.amateurgourmet.com/2011/10/how-to-support-yourself-as-a-food-blogger.html.

Robinson, Eugene. 2011. "Chris Christie's Big Problem." *Washington Post*, September 30. Accessed October 1, 2011. http://www.washingtonpost.com/opinions/chris-christies-big-problem/2011/09/29/gIQAAL7J8K_story.html.

Robinson, Lynne. 2009. "The Art of Food Blogging." *The Times*, February 17. Accessed February 5, 2011. http://www.timesonline.co.uk/tol/life_and_style/food_and_drink/real_food/article5753558.ece.

Rogers, Felisa. 2012. "Why Americans Sing about Food." *Salon*, January 8. Accessed January 10, 2012. http://www.salon.com/2012/01/08/why_americans_sing_about_food/.

Romenesko, Jim. 2008. "Is It Wrong for a Food Critic to Hire Local Chefs to Cater Her Wedding?" Poynter, October 9. Accessed October 2, 2011. http://www.poynter.org/latest-news/romenesko/91973/is-it-wrong-for-a-food-critic-to-hire-local-chefs-to-cater-her-wedding/.

Rosen, Jay. 2011. "The Twisted Psychology of Bloggers vs. Journalists: My Talk at South By Southwest." *Press Think*, March 12.. Accessed June 3, 2011. http://pressthink.org/2011/02/the-psychology-of-bloggers-vs-journalists-my-talk-at-south-by-southwest/..

Rousseau, Signe. 2012. *Food Media: Celebrity Chefs and the Politics of Everyday Interference.* Oxford: Berg.

Rushkoff, Douglas. 2002. "The Internet is Not Killing Off Conversation but Actively Encouraging It." In *We've Got Blog*, edited by John Rodzvilla, 116–88. Cambridge, MA: Perseus.

Sagon, Candy. 2005. "New Magazines Rewrite the Book On How to Cook." *Washington Post*, July 6. Accessed July 21, 2005. http://www.washingtonpost.com/wp-dyn/content/article/2005/07/05/AR2005070500330.html.

Salkin, Allen. 2007. "Sharp Bites." *New York Times*, February 4. Accessed February 7, 2009. http://www.nytimes.com/2007/02/04/fashion/04bloggers.html.

Santopietro, Jill. 2011. "Can an iPhone App Change the Way We Eat?" *Chow*, January 20. Accessed March 29, 2011. http://www.chow.com/food-news/71235/can-an-iphone-app-change-the-way-we-eat/.

Satran, Joe. 2011. "Celebrity Chef Restaurants: The Rise Of The Emperor-Chefs." *Huffington Post*, September 26. Accessed October 2, 2011. http://www.huffingtonpost.com/2011/09/26/celebrity-chef-restaurants-jean-georges-todd-english_n_974745.html.

Scalzi, John. 2011. "DeKloutifying." Whatever, November 14. Accessed November 16, 2011. http://whatever.scalzi.com/2011/11/14/dekloutifying/.

Shelasky, Alyssa. 2011. "Anthony Bourdain Is the Total Package." Grub Street New York, November 7. Accessed November 7, 2011. http://newyork.grubstreet.com/2011/11/anthony-bourdain-nude-pics-skinny-dipping.html.

Sheraton, Mimi. 2007. "Restaurateur Bites Critic: The Food Fight between Frank Bruni and Jeffrey Chodorow." *Slate*, February 24. Accessed February 26, 2007. http://www.slate.com/id/2160474/.

Shilcutt, Katharine. 2010. "Has the 'Foodie' Backlash Begun?" *Houston Press*, August 9. Accessed September 2, 2010. http://blogs.houstonpress.com/eating/2010/08/has_the_foodie_backlash_begun.php.

Shirky, Clay. 2008. *Here Comes Everybody: The Power of Organizing Without Organizations.* New York: Penguin.

Shriver, Jerry. 2005. "Incredible & Edible: In Search of Extreme Cuisine." *USA Today*, December 7. Accessed June 20, 2007. http://www.usatoday.com/travel/destinations/2005-12-07-extreme-cuisine_x.htm.

Siegler, MG. 2011. "I Will Check My Phone At Dinner And You Will Deal With It." TechCrunch, February 21. Accessed May 2, 2011. http://techcrunch.com/2011/02/21/phones-at-dinner/.

Sietsema, Robert. 2010a. "Everyone Eats . . . But That Doesn't Make You a Restaurant Critic." *Columbia Journalism Review*, January/February. Accessed February 2, 2011. http://replay.web.archive.org/20100519194448/http://www.cjr.org/feature/everyone_eats.php.

———. 2010b. "An Open Letter to Josh Ozersky." *Village Voice*, June 23. Accessed August 5, 2010. http://blogs.villagevoice.com/forkintheroad/2010/06/an_open_letter.php.

———. 2011. "Yes, Foodies Are Ridiculous. But Then So Is B. R. Myers!" *Village Voice*, February 10. Accessed February 12, 2011. http://blogs.villagevoice.com/forkintheroad/2011/02/yes_foodies_are.php.

Simon, Herbert A. 1978. "Rationality as Process and as Product of Thought." *The American Economic Review* 68(2), (Papers and Proceedings of the Ninetieth Annual Meeting of the American Economic Association): 1–16.

Singel, Ryan. 2011. "Google Recipe Search Cooks Up Next Gen of Search." *Wired*, February 24. Accessed June 12, 2011. http://www.wired.com/epicenter/2011/02/google-recipe-semantic.

Slater, Lydia. 2009. "Chef Julia Child, Her Book–and the Bored Wife Who Dished up a Global Hit." *The Daily Mail*, September 4. Accessed September 7, 2009. http://www.dailymail.co.uk/femail/food/article-1211005/Chef-Julia-Child-book--bored-wife-dished-global-hit.html.

Slayton, Joyce. 2011. "Stand Up OpenTable and It Will Dump Your Ass." *Chow*, September 21. Accessed October 10, 2011. http://www.chow.com/food-news/91666/stand-up-opentable-and-it-will-dump-your-ass/.

Smith, Andrew. 2007. "Copyrighting Recipes." Listserv Communication: ASFS (Association for the Study of Food and Society), January 8.

Smith, Catharine. 2011. "Foursquare Caters To Foodies With Mario Batali Partnership." *Huffington Post*, February 23. Accessed March 15, 2011. http://www.huffingtonpost.com/2011/02/23/foursquares-mario-batali-badge_n_827018.html.

Smith, Emily. 2011. "Much a Twitter About Alton." Eatocracy, October 24. Accessed October 30, 2011. http://eatocracy.cnn.com/2011/10/24/much-a-twitter-about-alton-brown/.

Solove, Daniel. 2004. *The Digital Person: Technology and Privacy in the Information Age.* New York: New York University Press.

———. 2007. *The Future of Reputation: Gossip, Rumor, and Privacy on the Internet.* New Haven, CT: Yale University Press.

———. 2011. "Why Privacy Matters Even if You Have 'Nothing to Hide.'" *The Chronicle Review*, May 15. Accessed May 20, 2011. http://chronicle.com/article/Why-Privacy-Matters-Even-if/127461/.

Spotswood, Beth. 2011. "Getting Dumped By OpenTable.com." Tourist Trapped, San Francisco Gate, September 19. Accessed October 12, 2011. http://blog.sfgate.com/culture/2011/09/19/tourist-trapped-getting-dumped-by-opentable-com/.

Stein, Jeannine. 2011. "Tailored Text Messages Might Help Teens Lose Weight." *Los Angeles Times*, August 30. Accessed September 10, 2011. http://www.latimes.com/health/boostershots/la-heb-teen-texting-weight-loss-20110830,0,5332591.story.

Stratten, Scott. 2012. "Worst Use of Social Media of 2012: Boners BBQ." UnMarketing, January 10. Accessed January 14, 2012. http://www.unmarketing.com/2012/01/10/worst-use-of-social-media-of-2012-boners-bbq/.

Sundar, S. Shyam, Edwards, Heidi Hatfield, Hu, Yifeng, and Stavrositu, Carmen. 2007. "Blogging for Better Health: Putting the 'Public' Back in Health." In *Blogging, Citizenship, and the Future of Media*, edited by Mark Tremayne, 83–102. New York: Routledge.

Sunstein, Cass R. 2010. "Believing False Rumours." In *The Offensive Internet*, edited by Saul Levmore and Martha C. Nussbaum, 91–106. Cambridge, MA: Harvard University Press.

Suthivarakom, Ganda. 2011a. "How Food Blogging Changed My Life." *Saveur*, May 9. Accessed May 11, 2011. http://www.saveur.com/article/Kitchen/How-Food-Blogging-Changed-My-Life.

———. 2011b. "A Brief History of Food Blogs." *Saveur*, May 9. Accessed May 11, 2011. http://www.saveur.com/article/Kitchen/A-Brief-Food-Blog-Timeline.

Sylva, Bob. 2007. "The Internet is cooking." *Sacramento Bee*, May 23. Accessed May 30, 2007. http://web.archive.org/web/20070616203909/http://www.sacbee.com/taste/story/189876.html.

Sytsma, Alan. 2011. "Simpsons Executive Producer Matt Selman on the Show's Upcoming Foodie Episode." Grub Street New York, November 7. Accessed November 12, 2011. http://newyork.grubstreet.com/2011/11/simpsons-food-episode-preview.html.

Tedeschi, Bob. 2007. "Readers Are Key Ingredient as Virtual Kitchen Heats Up." *New York Times*, June 25. Accessed June 27, 2007. http://www.nytimes.com/2007/06/25/technology/25ecom.html.

TheCriticalCouple. 2010. "Marcus Wareing at the Berkeley: a very disappointing service." The Critical Couple, October 25. Accessed November 6, 2010. http://www.thecriticalcouple.com/1/post/2010/10/marcus-wareing-at-the-berkeley-a-very-disappointing-service.html.

Thelin, Emily Kaiser. 2011. "The Omnivorous Michael Pollan (Interview)." *Wall Street Journal*, November 19. Accessed November 22, 2011.http://online.wsj.com/article/SB10001424052970204224604577032221097635472.html.

Thompson, Jonathan. 2007. "The Gospel According to Gordon Ramsey [sic] (Warning: It May Be Enough to Put You Off Your Breakfast)." *Independent*, April 29. Accessed May 4, 2007. http://news.independent.co.uk/uk/this_britain/article2494229.ece.

Tossell, Ivor. 2010. "Copyright Scandal cooks up online frontier justice." *Globe and Mail*, November 8. Accessed January 10, 2011. http://www.theglobeandmail.com/news/technology/digital-culture/ivor-tossell/copyright-scandal-cooks-up-online-frontier-justice/article1790781/.

Tversky, Amos, and Kahneman, Daniel. 1974. "Judgments under Uncertainty: Heuristics and Biases." *Science* 185: 1124–31.

Ungerleider, Neal. 2011. "Chop Sue-y: Benihana Takes Blogger to Court Over Poor Review." *Fast Company*, February 3. Accessed March 10, 2011. http://www.fastcompany.com/1723689/benihana-kuwait-lawsuit-mark-makhou-mike-servo.

Villarica, Hans. 2011. "10 Things We Can Learn from Your Health-Related Twitter Rants." *Atlantic*, July 15. Accessed August 10, 2011. http://www.theatlantic.com/life/archive/2011/07/10-things-we-can-learn-from-your-health-related-twitter-rants/242002/.

Wasserman, Todd. 2011. "What's Behind the Food Photography Trend?" Mashable, May 10. Accessed May 11, 2011. http://mashable.com/2011/05/09/foodtography-infographic/.

Wells, Pete. 2006. "New Era of the Recipe Burglar." *Food & Wine*. Accessed January 5, 2010. http://www.foodandwine.com/articles/new-era-of-the-recipe-burglar.

Wendell, Sarah. 2010a. "Judith Griggs: The Google Is Our Friend, Not Hers." Smart Bitches, Trashy Books, November 4. Accessed January 10, 2011. http://www.smartbitchestrashybooks.com/index.php/weblog/comments/judith-griggs-the-google-is-our-friend-not-hers/.

———. 2010b. "Lessons Learned from Cook's Source." Smart Bitches, Trashy Books, November 10. Accessed January 10, 2011.http://www.smartbitchestrashybooks.com/index.php/weblog/comments/lessons-learned-from-cooks-source/.

Wells, Pete. 2006. "New Era of the Recipe Burglar." *Food & Wine*. Accessed January 5, 2010. http://www.foodandwine.com/articles/new-era-of-the-recipe-burglar.

West, Patrick. 2007. "YouTube vs Television." *Spiked*, November 9. Accessed November 12, 2007. http://www.spiked-online.com/index.php?/site/article/4062/.

White, Trevor. 2007. *Kitchen Con: Writing on the Restaurant Racket*. Edinburgh: Mainstream Publishing.

Whitelocks, Sadie. 2012. "Cake Replaces Chicken as UK's Most Searched-for Food Term Thanks to TV Baking Shows." *The Daily Mail*, January 9. Accessed January 10, 2012. http://www.dailymail.co.uk/femail/article-2084157/Cake-replaces-chicken-UKs-searched-food-term-thanks-TV-baking-shows.html.

Wilder, Andrew. 2011. "Has Food Blogging Jumped the Shark?" *BlogTutor*, November 20. Accessed November 22, 2011. http://blogtutor.com/2011/11/has-food-blogging-jumped-the-shark/.

Williams, Zoe. 2011. "El Bulli closes: Farewell parmesan frozen air . . . " *The Guardian*, July 30. Accessed July 30, 2011. http://www.guardian.co.uk/lifeandstyle/2011/jul/30/el-bulli-closes-ferran-adria.

Willis, Virginia. 2009. "Julia and Julie: Yes, The Swap Is Intentional." *Virginia Willis Culinary Productions*, July 11. Accessed March 8, 2011. http://virginiawillis.wordpress.com/2009/07/11/julia-and-julie-yes-the-swap-is-intentional/.

————. 2011. "Sour Grapes and Sweet Maine Lobster Chowder." *Virginia Willis Culinary Productions*, August 26. Accessed September 5, 2011. http://virginiawillis.wordpress.com/2011/08/26/sour-grapes-and-sweet-maine-lobster-chowder/.

Wilson, Jenny L., Peebles, Rebecka, Hardy, Kristina K., and Litt, Iris F. 2006. "Surfing for Thinness: A Pilot Study of Pro-Eating Disorder Web Site Usage in Adolescents with Eating Disorders." *Pediatrics* 118(6): 1635–43.

Zuckerman, Ethan. 2008. "Homophily, Serendipity, Xenophilia." My Heart's in Accra, April 25. Accessed July 2, 2011. http://www.ethanzuckerman.com/blog/2008/04/25/homophily-serendipity-xenophilia/.

Index

About the Author

Signe Rousseau teaches critical literacy at the University of Cape Town, South Africa. She is the author of *Food Media: Celebrity Chefs and the Politics of Everyday Interference* (2012) and is active in the discussion of the food scene on both sides of the Atlantic, particularly of how food media celebrities influence the perception of food and eating in an obesity crisis.